Early one Morning

This catalogue is published by the whitechapel Art Gallery on the occasion of the exhibition,
Early one Morning, 6 July – 8 september 2002

Exhibition curated by **Iwona Blazwick** and **Andrea Tarsia**
organised by **candy stobbs**

catalogue designed by **SMITH**
Printed in the united Kingdom by **Dexters**
whitechapel installation views by **Anthony weller**

ISBN: 0 85488 130 1

Published by whitechapel Art Gallery
80–82 whitechapel High street, London E1 7QX, UK
Tel: +44 (0)20 7522 7888
Fax: +44 (0)20 7377 1685
Email: info@whitechapel.org
www.whitechapel.org

Early one Morning
British Art Now

whitechapel Art Gallery
2002

shahin Afrassiabi
claire Barclay
Jim Lambie
Eva Rothschild
Gary webb

gary webb

installation view previous pages

mirage of loose change, 2001 opposite above

sound of the blue light, 2002 opposite below

heart and soul, 2000 and **matte module, 2002** top

claire вarclay
collars for woodseers, **2002** previous pages, opposite and above

shahin ᴀfrassiabi
ᴅisplay with ᴛable, 2002 previous pages

ᴅisplay with ʟinoleum ᴛiles, 2002

shelf ᴅisplay with clock ʀadio, 2002

ᴀmp, 2002

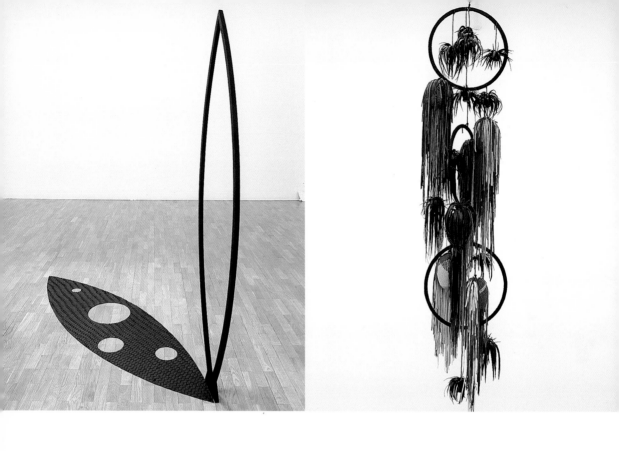

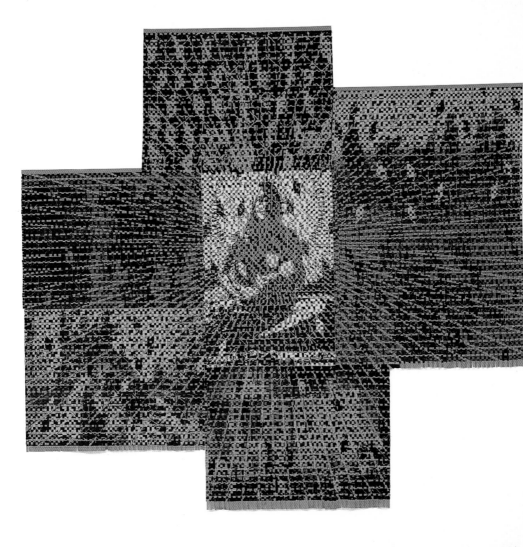

...
proper
abstract
sculpture
doesn't
usually
come
accessorized
...

**Alex
Farquharson**[1]

New British sculpture in the 21st century
Iwona Blazwick

video and photography have, through the 1990s, proved the medium of choice in contemporary art. If the experience of art has therefore been predominantly two dimensional, image based and retinal, perhaps it's not surprising to find a new generation turning again to the three dimensional, material and phenomenal pleasures of sculpture. But it is sculpture which parts company with the figurative installations and *mise-en-scènes* that have dominated much European and American practice in the late 20th century. It returns instead to the earlier trajectories of Modernism – to the realms of abstraction.

The title of this show expresses not only the quietly thrilling imminence of a new dawn, a sense of optimism and curiosity bound up in looking to the future; it also embraces the past. *Early one Morning* pays tribute to the radical opening up of postwar sculpture encapsulated by Anthony Caro's eponymous work of 1962 (pp. 32-33). In its abstract, open-ended structure, dazzling use of colour and industrial technique it prefigures a new tendency, emerging at the outset of the 21st century. What are its characteristics?

On first sight the work featured here doesn't offer up a mirror, to ourselves or the world around us. Resolutely non-figurative, it asserts an abstract presence, through juxtapositions of colour, volume and texture. If 'real' objects do make an appearance then their function has been blurred or customised; they have lost contact with the outside world and been indoctrinated into the internal logic of the work of art. The sculptures featured here are assemblages. Their components may be arranged centripetally, sucked together as if unable to resist some inner gravitational force. Some are stacked and piled to lean and balance in a casual, even precarious interdependence; others leach out of their surroundings, sprouting like fungus in the corner of a room, or cascading from a beam like a tropical creeper. In this assembly of materials the artists oscillate between the architectonic logic of construction techniques and the biomorphic procedures of organic, cellular growth.

Dissatisfied with the readymade and with an eye to the marvels of manufacture or the home spun intricacies of the craft object, the artists typically combine making things themselves with subcontracting various components. Taking the irrational as their blueprint, a dream or a doodle can provide the starting point for a precise technical specification that can then be fabricated. The making of works may incorporate an element of chance, the unpredictable intervention of a third party: the idiosyn-crasies and unconscious customisations of the tool and dye worker, the glass blower or craftsman offer a rogue element that guides the evolution of the final piece. It is this agglomeration of highly crafted components with creative misreadings, the inherent qualities of a material and its wilful distortion and mutation, that contributes to these works' non unitary, multi-perspectival quality.

Difficult to define as strictly sculpture or installation, the scale of works draws on the domestic and is evolved in relation to a gallery environ-ment. In fact scale reveals that these apparently abstract pieces make anthropomorphic, cultural and even political references. The body is everywhere, but by implication – the sensual tactility of suede, the sexual innuendo of holes and spikes, the cavities and passageways that propose the viewer become performer.

The choice of materials reveals a genesis of making inspired simply by what comes to hand – things that might be lying around a bedroom, picked up in the charity shop, hardware store or crafts supplier. We might encounter a camouflaged loudspeaker (its sheer bulk proclaiming its obsolescence in the age of micro technologies); a modest but brand new section of MDF shelving complete with adjustable brackets; or some intri-cately woven strips of soft leather in a range of autumnal colours. These are not the organic or 'poor' fragments of Arte Povera; neither do they have the knowingly repulsive consumer sheen of so called 'neo-geo' hyper-realism. From the do-it-yourself convenience of modern construc-tion materials to the Arts and crafts revivalism of natural fibres, the artists carefully select the material signifiers of lost utopias.

In trying to define this new sculpture, it is also impossible not to think of painting. The works featured in *Early one Morning* move between a phe-nomenal experience of mass, volume and plane and a retinal impact triggered by colour and surface. There are links with American minimalists such as Donald Judd and Dan Flavin in that the colour is not applied but is integral to the materials used, whether they be corner– shop plastic shopping bags, or flourescent light bulbs. A 2D picture plane is set up within which materials perform to their full optical capacity. Transparent glassy surfaces set up transparencies and reflections, alongside dense matt or fluffy lumps of stuff in shades of mud. Complimentary colours project and recede. Bouncy cartoon-like silhouettes are juxtaposed with the ephemeral provisionality of taking a line for a walk. The thickness of a sheet of Perspex is used to refract a beam of coloured light.

Throughout this work there is in fact a very orthodox truth to materials; the size, shape and positioning of an object will often be dictated by its inherent qualities. However the materials themselves are often synthetic, capable of infinite mutation and plasticity. They are also cultural, emotional and psychic signifiers. Their Proustian impact can be triggered by colour: silver and black may have a far off echo in a 1970s album cover; day-glo pink and yellow reinvoke the aesthetics of psychedelia while macrame ropes transport us into the heart of a hippy commune. Forms may wear their art historical genealogies on their sleeves – a planar assembly of rectangles refers to constructivism, while a smoothly curved expanse of plastic is reminiscent of New Generation abstraction. Rather than representing the world outside, a shape might simply hint at a 1950s ornament itself inspired by a seahorse.

Material and texture might trigger feelings of security, nostalgia or a sense of dread: a woven mass of fluffy white fibres seems comforting until juxtaposed with a smooth metal spike. The impact of the visual is overtaken by the high speed hit of sound or smell, added extras that deliver an instantaneous riff of memory, triggering associations of pleasure and pain which go beyond language.

These sculptures and installations immerse artist and viewer in a physical universe that we have been accustomed to occupying only as spectators and consumers. They go back to the profusion and promise of modern life in both its dominant and counter-cultural forms. Accepting the failures of both, the artists of *Early one Morning* reignite their latent poetic and transformative potential with a bright contemporary sensibility.

Early one Morning combines recent works with new pieces conceived and created for the Whitechapel Art Gallery. The realisation of the show was helped immeasurably by support and advice from Susanna Beaumont, Detmar Blow, Sadie Coles, Pauline Daly, Niamh Doyle, Ben Harman, Andrew Hawes, Stephen Hepworth, Colin Ledwith, Kitia, Rania Kontos, Francis Lamb, Andrew Marsh, Jake Millar, Kirsty Ogg, Steven Pippet, Danny Saunders, Stuart Shave, Ralph Tait, Jim Valentine, Toby Webster, Rachel Williams and James Winrow. We also wish to thank Mary Horlock, Judith Nesbitt and Chris Stephens at Tate Britain for agreeing to collaborate with us on their display of New Generation sculptors by mounting a parallel display of two dimensional works by *Early one Morning* contributors.

The show could not have been realised without the generosity of lenders; our thanks to the Arts Council, the British Council, Sadie Coles HQ, The Approach, Doggerfisher, Modern Art, The Modern Institute, Vilma Gold, Anita and Poju Zabludowicz and those who wish to remain anonymous. We also gratefully acknowledge the financial support and enlightened patronage of The Henry Moore Foundation and Exhibition Circle; and the sponsorship in kind of the old Truman Brewery and San Miguel beer.

A historical context for this publication has been given by Mary Horlock's essay on British sculpture in the 1960s, complementing Andrea Tarsia's analysis of five contemporaries. The book itself is beautifully designed by Stuart Smith.

It also includes the voices of the artists speaking about sources, creative processes and intentions. We are most grateful to Shahin Afrassiabi, Claire Barclay, Jim Lambie, Eva Rothschild and Gary Webb for their energy, commitment and creativity in contributing to this book; and in present-ing a constellation of remarkable, stand alone installations which together propose a paradigm shift in contemporary art.

1   Alex Farquharson, 'Flim flam man', *Frieze*, London, May 2002

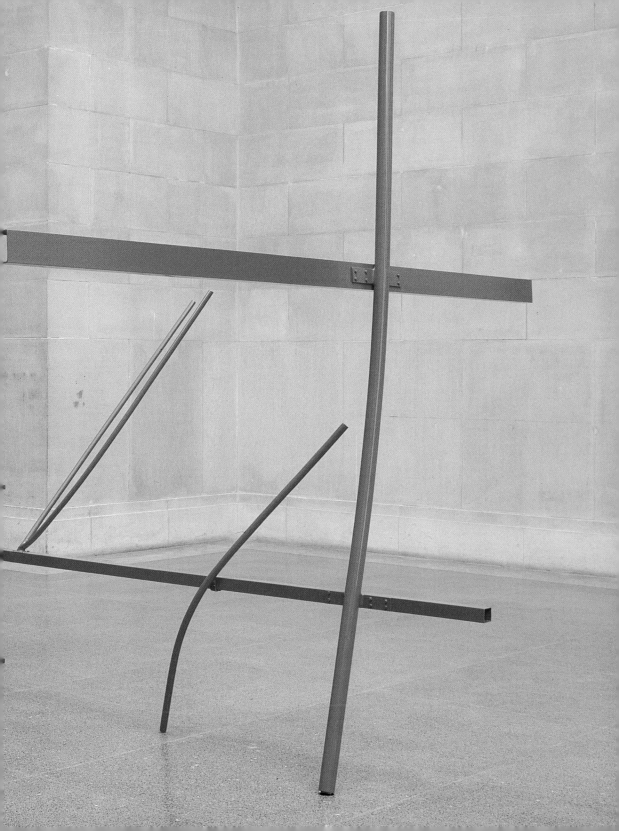

For
a
long
while
painting,
in
many
ways,
has
tried
to
approximate
to
the
condition
of
sculpture
which,
in
turn,
has
pushed
increasingly
towards
the
special
plasticity,
fluidity
and
freedom
of
painting.
**Bryan
Robertson**[1]

Tra-La-La – British sculpture in the sixties
Mary Horlock

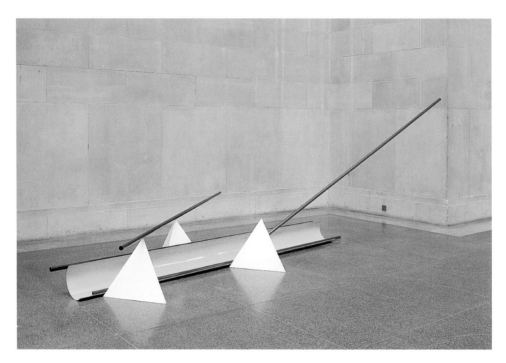

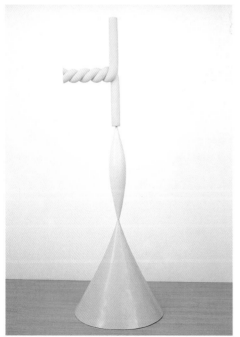

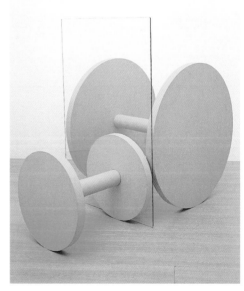

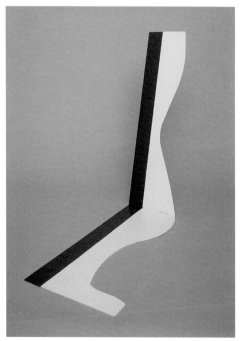

In 1965 Anthony Caro's *Early one Morning*, 1962 (pp. 32-33) was included in the exhibition *British sculpture in the 60s* at the Tate. Despite being constructed from steel pipes, girders and plates the structure of this sculpture seems divested of solidity: flat planes and curving lines are locked into a fragile equilibrium that defies gravity, with a unifying coat of bright red paint enhancing the sense of weightlessness. Some critics saw in this sculpture a reference to the act of painting, with the red rectangle at one end representing an easel, but *Early one Morning* remains defiantly abstract. As Michael Fried argued it is like, 'not gesture exactly but the *efficacy* of gesture, like certain music or poetry.'[2]

The same year that *Early one Morning* was shown at the Tate, nine young sculptors were selected for the *New Generation* exhibition at the Whitechapel Gallery, the second of a series of shows that focused on emerging talent. The first in 1964 had been dedicated to painting, and 1965 was the turn of sculpture. Six of the selected sculptors - David Annesley, Michael Bolus, Phillip King, Tim Scott, William Tucker and Isaac Witkin - studied at St Martin's School of Art, where Caro taught. Encouraged by Caro's example they had begun to formulate 'a radically new and different concept of sculpture' which constituted something of a 'revolution'[3] when exhibited at the Whitechapel. These new works were visually and physically arresting; abstract in shape and confrontational in scale, standing squarely on the floor and echoing human proportions. Brightly coloured and made using steel, fibreglass, or plastic (indeed anything other than bronze) they represented a complete break with the sculpture of the previous decade.

The *New Generation* show at the Whitechapel somewhat eclipsed the Tate's *British sculpture* survey. Predictably, the Tate selection contained only a few surprises, and many of the exhibiting artists - Michael Ayrton, Reg Butler and Bernard Meadows - were still working in bronze. The introductory text in the catalogue adopts a somewhat defensive tone on their behalf, acknowledging, 'the New Generation at the Whitechapel represents a real challenge to almost all of them in that this group of the younger sculptors so clearly rejects much of what their elders stand for.'[4] Of course, there was some common (albeit shifting) ground between the two generations and exhibitions, visible not just in caro's *Early one Morning* but also in the work of william тurnbull. тurnbull was represented by several elegantly abstract steel sculptures that rose straight up from the floor, a significant departure from his earlier work in bronze.

jumping ahead to 2002 the work of phillip кing and his contemporaries is now on display at тate вritain, alongside work by caro and тurnbull. тhus, the current, up-dated version of *вritish sculpture in the 6os* presented by тate вritain encapsulates the transformative trends that came to the fore back then. it is a riot of painted sheet steel, aluminium, wood and fibreglass. вold, impermeable forms sprawl across the floor and project out into space. тhese sculptures still look disconcertingly fresh and 'new' – resistant to the confining hold of history – but they can offer something of a context for the current group of younger artists now selected to exhibit at the whitechapel. тhe work of shahin аfrassiabi, claire вarclay, jim сambie, еva кothschild and gary webb is informed by the legacy of the новем генеration: an interest in painting (the manipulation of colour and surface); the desire to test out synthetic materials (materials associated with industry and manufacturing); a concern with scale and plasticity (but a resistance to the monumental) and a keen regard for architecture and design. such themes and ideas resonate across the generations.

*

то вridget кiley, *Early one Morning* looked like 'a painting that has been pulled out of its frame'[5] and caro would be the first to acknowledge that by 1960, sculpture was entering an area very close to that of painting. нis discussions with the аmerican art critic and champion of high мodernism clement greenberg had helped clarify his ideas about sculpture – "greenberg came in with a clear eye and a clear mind"[6]. аrguing for 'purity' and 'reduction', greenberg encouraged caro to consider how abstract art could trigger emotions and experiences directly, citing the example of 'colour field' painters such as кenneth нoland, мorris сouis and jules olitski. shortly after this, caro visited the u.s. and encountered нoland's and сouis's canvases firsthand. '... i realised that i had nothing to lose by throwing out history... аmerica made me see that there are no barriers and no regulations... There is tremendous freedom in knowing that your only limitations in sculpture or painting are whether it carries its intention or not, not whether it's 'Art'"[7] And so caro changed his habits: he gave up traditional techniques of carving and modelling, abandoned figure-based work and started 'assembling' his sculptures from steel. Through an open, improvisatory process - a process many likened to collage - he created a loose, abstract syntax for sculpture, as represented by *Early one Morning*.

writing in the *New Generation* catalogue a few years later Ian Dunlop pointed out that caro was not alone in finding a model and paradigm in American painting: 'Painting has influenced the look, as opposed to the spirit, of this sculpture; though possibly that too... American painters... have all had their effect'. Indeed, in 1960 Phillip King had seen American painting as offering 'a sort of message of hope and optimism'[8] and later acknowledged that it was: "other painters, rather than sculptors, who interested me."[9] Likewise, Michael Bolus, Tim Scott and william Tucker would enthusiastically list the painters who influenced their work, from Henri Matisse to Robert Motherwell. writing about King and his colleagues, the whitechapel's director Bryan Robertson noted the connection with American painting, but also saw close ties with young British painters. He recalled how, in the previous *New Generation* exhibition, Paul Huxley had defined his position as a painter: 'painting can only be enlightening by posing questions and making reconnaissance trips rather than supplying answers. we become more wise by not knowing.'[10] Robertson identified a similar sensibility in the young sculptors as well as a strong formal resemblance between contemporary British painting and sculpture.

Already, the impact of American abstract painting on British painting had been profound. A painter himself, william Turnbull had taken on the developments in America ahead of caro's discovery of Noland's stained canvases, and in the late 50s begun to paint large monochrome canvases, first thickly worked with a palette knife, then more thinly painted. Turnbull had come together with painters like Bernard cohen, Robyn Denny, John Hoyland and Richard smith in the *situation* exhibitions of 1960 and 1961, and American abstract painting was the model for them.

making art with a new focus and daring they left out all 'reference to events outside the painting'.[11] тhere was a closeness developing between them and the sculptors working and teaching at st martin's. david annesley, michael bolus, phillip king, тim scott, william tucker and isaac witkin engaged with caro in this context. тhe enquiring attitude that caro brought to sculpture as a discipline was enhanced by the contributions of bernard cohen and тurnbull amongst others. тurnbull's insistence that caro was represented in the second *situation* exhibition in 1961 with *sculpture 1* in itself speaks volumes. sculpture was taking on both 'the spirit' and 'the look' of painting.

'new materials, new concepts...'[12]

many of the american artists who came after jackson pollock – painters like elsworth kelly and frank stella – reacted against his expressive style of painting, preferring a cooler approach and a simpler repertoire of forms. similarly, a new generation of sculptors following Henry moore and alberto giacometti rejected the expressive surface of bronze and the traditional practices of modelling and carving (practices that emphasised the hand of the artist). instead, they chose materials that would make for a smooth, 'finished', more impersonal type of sculpture.

in terms of sculptural practice, welding had only enjoyed a brief history so far: in the work of pablo picasso and julio gonzález and latterly in the sculptures of david smith. caro's recommendation that a welding shop be set up at st.martin's proved auspicious and annesley, bolus and тucker all began to experiment with steel, sourcing raw material from scrapyards. annesley echoed caro's view when he remarked that steel was 'neutral – just stuff' and 'the most flexible, durable material you could use.'[13] its potential is apparent in a work like *swing low*, 1964 (p. 37 above) where hard-edged rectilinear shapes combine with rippling lines. annesley emphasised both the fluidity and rigidity of the steel. тhe strong linear profile of his sculptures suggests painting or drawing in space. тhat steel was light enough and strong enough to define and articulate space was something bolus explored in *11th sculpture*, 1963, where a series of connecting steel plates rise up before us. The work embodies a physical sensation - that of seeming to resist gravity and rise from the ground - in purely abstract terms. His later *1st sculpture*, 1967-8 (p. 36 above) is also wonderfully buoyant, with clean lines expanding outwards.

Besides steel, new materials like plastics, fibreglass and resin were readily available. Adopting these materials allowed younger artists to distance themselves from caro's teaching and practice, whilst also offering the chance to develop new sculptural forms. King was the first to work directly in plastic and fibreglass, and this was more than simply a technical breakthrough since the shapes he made would have been difficult or impossible to achieve through carving or welding. The sculptures King produced in the early '60s generally had an enclosed, concentrated presence, an object-like character that was quite different from caro's open, unbounded forms. *ghengis Khan*, 1963, for example, resembles a mountain or cone. There is a sense of simultaneous implosion and explosion, bursting forth above and trickling out underneath: 'it's a continuous surface, in that the parts, although spreading out away from the centre, are all flowing in a continuous form.'[14] *ghengis Khan* relates to *Rosebud*, 1962 and *And the Birds began to sing*, 1964: all three being comprised of sheets that wrap around each other making cone shapes. The fantastic, vertical form of *Tra-La-La*, 1963 (p. 36 below left) came about at roughly the same time. The solidity of its rounded base supports the fluid, twisting pipes that rise up into the air. There is a touch of surrealism in this image and the title is wonderfully apt: conveying something that is playful, weightless and free.

Tim scott's imagery was often just as fantastical. Through his architectural training he was drawn to experiment with quasi-geometric forms, and to testing out the latest synthetic materials on the market. He came to use polyurethane, glass, fibreglass and wood, and often combined different materials in a single work, as in *Peach wheels*, 1961 (p. 36 below right), where a sheet of glass stands upright, separating two sets of wooden wheels, identical but for their scale and orientation - a strange asymmetry. scott began working with fibreglass because it was practical: "it was an easy way of making a large solid, which was hollow and light" but he soon moved on to experimenting with plastic: "when you make things in fibreglass you have to finish them, to paint them with something, because otherwise they would be a dirty brown colour. I therefore started painting the surfaces... I found paint to be very limited... so I looked to other methods of incorporating colour. It occurred to me that acrylic sheets are literally pieces of colour, solid colour."[15] And so colour became integral to the material, resulting in works like *quadreme*, 1966, where a vivid blue, yellow and orange define volume and form.

'colour is perhaps the most obviously new thing about this sculpture, with a variety of uses. It can set the mood of a piece, it can help underline some feature in the structure that needs emphasising, but more often than not it acts like a skin.'[16]
Ian Dunlop

The transformative power of colour had already been demonstrated in painting. The surfaces of these steel and fibreglass sculptures were like blank canvases and colour came in partly because the materials demanded it. It took on a role it had previously only had in painting, although individual artists developed it in different directions. caro started using it as a way of neutralising the 'industrial' effect that steel might otherwise have had; it added to the sense of illusion. As a painter, colour was always a primary concern for Turnbull, and when he began to make stripped down abstract forms he painted them to reinforce their structure. He acknowledged colour had an emotive force but used it factually rather than expressively: 'I don't want colour to be expressive separately from material or structure.'[17]

of a younger generation, King and scott were perhaps more eager to grasp colour's power of suggestion - how it could energise and dematerialise the sculptural form. King readily admitted:

"sculptors in the past were little interested in using colour as they tended to emphasise the quality of the material. surface texture portrayed the character of the material and the working tools of the artist rather like brushmark in a painting. то paint on top seemed to give a concealing skin to all this. тhe answer to using colour for me, then, was to remove surface texture, work within a more neutral and smoother surface. working in materials that had no history and were intractable like plastics helped… colour comes in towards the end of making a work, but I feel it is subconsciously carried in one's mind throughout the working process, as stored up experience, and is a definite affecting force… colour also plays an important role in extending the symbolic meaning of the shapes and clarifying imagery."[18]

тhe purple of a sculpture like *ghengis кhan* is regal and imposing, whilst the green of *green streamer*, 1970 suggests a landscape. speaking of *Rosebud*, the sculpture that preceded *ghengis кhan* he said: 'тhe pink I used was colour no longer subservient to the material but something on its own, to do with surface and skin really. using pink, the most unsculptural colour of the lot, was another form of manifesto…'[19] кing would also counteract too specific a reference to nature by using non-associative synthetic colour. тhis could be said for the confectionery pinks of *тra-La-La*. In this work, кing also varied the surfaces, with a shiny finish at the base and a matt coat at the tip. similarly, scott (who cited мatisse's late cut-outs as a key influence) made the wood of *peach wheels* seem softer by painting it a luscious pink, and using a matt paint, so the colour really appeared to sink in. нe said: "when one started using colours on sculpture, it seemed to me unsatisfactory to choose it arbitrarily, so I started to get interested in colour as such, to try to use colour in a constructive way…"[20] A lyrical, playful mood could be evoked though strong and unexpected colours. мichael вolus's approach was equally painterly: In *1st sculpture*, 1967-8 the protruding lines of pure colour are supported by white pyramids, the white supports rest on the floor, establishing a break between the strong colours and the ground, as in some of Frank stella's stripe paintings. тhe colours are restricted to red, yellow, blue and white, recalling вolus's admiration for мondrian. Ian Dunlop wrote that вolus 'has broken down the barriers between painting and sculpture' and 'has discovered a new way of sculpting which enables him to explore an area previously reserved for painters like Richard smith and Frank stella.'[21]

of course, dunlop and others were quick to draw analogies with painting because this sculpture had broken with its own past so significantly - the connections with painting seemed more direct. And the parallels in terms of style and structure were only strengthened with a consideration of scale.

'The basic and recurring feature of all this sculpture is probably its size. The works are the size they are because they could be no other. It so happens that the sizes these young sculptors prefer is not particularly commodious… The sculpture in this exhibition is to be seen as sculpture only, and that is its sole function and challenge.'[22]

scale was a crucial concern for painters and sculptors in the early 1960s. size mattered. The paintings that were shown in the first *situation* exhibition in 1960 had to be abstract, but also - and significantly - they had to measure over 30 square feet. Moreover, they had to be experienced at close range - 'standing back is not the way into the big picture,' wrote Lawrence Alloway.[23] This insistence on scale and closeness, voiced by painters like Richard smith, was reiterated by caro when discussing his approach to making sculpture: "The advantage of making them where I couldn't stand back from them was that I used this limitation to prevent my falling back on my previous knowledge of balance and composition … I wanted to refrain from backing away and editing the work prematurely."[24] It was no longer just about the work of art; it was about its physical relationship to the viewer/artist. when encountering an artwork, the combination of physical actuality, optical impression and subjective experience was much discussed, by painters like Bernard cohen and by sculptors such as Philip King and william Tucker.

The physicality of Turnbull's sculpture is uncompromisingly direct. Turnbull believed that repeated units, when grouped together, could make for a stronger experience, hence the configurations of *5 x 1*, 1966 or *Transparent Tubes*, 1968 (p. 37 below right). In *5 x 1* each unit occupies its own space whilst forming a 'network'. The viewer can walk around the units, or through them, relate to them individually or as a group. similarly, all the sculptures exhibited in the *New Generation* show stood directly on the floor and occupied the same space as those who viewed them. 'The physical nature of the sculpture - the fact that it is first and foremost an object that occupies or invades our own space - is the prime factor to be reckoned with.'[25]

Phillip King later explained: 'I thought about things like my total skin area ... the volume of my body, my height and my reach... I was conscious of relating those physical proportions to my work.' He also said: 'Avoiding using a pedestal meant that making sculpture was like working with another person opposite you. Although I was making abstract work, it felt like a presence, or an alternative one, relating to me in some ways on a physical basis.'[26] Never is this clearer than in *Ghengis Khan*.

In common with Scott, Tucker believed that sculpture was now fulfilling the aesthetic and physical potential of architecture. Both made work on a scale that was far from ornamental. Making large works that relate to architecture was a bold and courageous statement and stridently non-commercial. A rare figure in British art at the time, Alistair MacAlpine bought many of these sculptures, acknowledging the dilemma he faced of "buying works that were too large to house, sold with the cautious words of a dealer, 'I am afraid I can never take a large piece back'."[27] Indeed, when MacAlpine gave 60 sculptures to the Tate, his wish that the collection be shown in its entirety could not be achieved. There was simply not enough space in the Gallery at the time. In the end, selected highlights were exhibited in a former drill hall off Tottenham Court Road in 1972.

*

Just as it was difficult to find the right space for New Generation sculpture then, so it has been difficult to situate it comfortably in art history ever since. That it related to architecture and design as well as painting was often debated, and this triggered some concern that 'pure' sculptural concerns were being diluted. Bryan Robertson recalled how at the time of the *New Generation* show in 1965 many critics would trivialise the work and 'write breathlessly of the new coloured sculpture in the same

gushing tones used to describe Mary Quant's miniskirts, or the new hair-
cuts, new colours in lipsticks, the Beatles and swinging London'.[28] Indeed,
several sculptors would soon narrow their practice, working in a single
material like steel later in the decade. Scott commented how welding
became the 'House style' of St. Martin's. Tucker turned to bronze.

Within a relatively short span of time the 'New Generation' artists became
a kind of orthodoxy that the next generation, represented by artists such
as Bruce McLean, Stuart Brisley, Richard Long and Barry Flanagan, would
rise up to challenge. McLean's performance of *There's a sculpture on my
shoulder* (first realised in 1970 and recently re-staged at the Whitechapel)
is proof of this transformation: we see the artist straining under pro-
jected images of New Generation sculptures, seemingly weighed down by
the tradition they represent. That McLean found a work like *Tra-La-La* to
be as cumbersome and conventional as a Henry Moore (who was targeted
in other performances) is telling. But this is to oversimplify events.
Working and teaching at St. Martin's, Caro and his colleagues initiated
and sustained a thorough enquiry into the nature of modern sculpture,
examining both the concept and process involved, re-evaluating the role
of the sculptor, and emphasising the relationship of the sculptor to the
material world. Benefiting from a long-term view, it is possible to see how
Caro and New Generation sculpture actually laid the ground for a broader
conceptual approach, which ultimately empowered artists like McLean
and Brisley. New Generation offered more than a widening range of materials, it offered new definitions as well.

In 1968 Phillip King had considered using polystyrene to create a kind of
installation in his solo show at the Whitechapel Gallery. Today, he incor-
porates diverse materials in his sculpture with the same enquiring spirit.
When asked about the lasting interest in New Generation sculpture he can
offer a succinct explanation: sculpture in the 60s had so many possibilities – and these possibilities are precisely reflected in today's practice,
after all "we are moving towards an age when our materials can be whatever we want them to be."[29]

1   Bryan Robertson, *New Generation* (ex cat), whitechapel Art Gallery, London 1965, p. 8
2   Michael Fried, 'Art and objecthood', first published in *Artforum*, no.5, New York June 1967, republished in *Art and objecthood: Essays and Reviews*, University of chicago Press, 1998, p. 162
3   Robertson, ibid, p. 8
4   Introduction, *British sculpture in the sixties* (ex cat), Tate Gallery, London 1965, n.p.
5   David Mellor, *the sixties art scene in london* (ex cat), Barbican Art Gallery, London 1993, p. 97
6   From 'Anthony caro – A Discussion with Peter Fuller' in Dieter Blume, *Anthony caro III: steel sculptures 1960-80*, cat raisonné, Galerie wentzel, cologne 1981, p. 38
7   *Gazette* Number 1, Graphis Press Limited, London 1961
8   Phillip King: 'Notes on sculpture', *studio International*, London, June 1968
9   Interview with David Mellor: 23 July 1991, repro in D. Mellor, ibid., p. 100
10 Robertson, ibid, p. 9
11 Roger coleman, *situation*, RBA Galleries, London, August 1960
12 Robertson, ibid, p. 9
13 David Annesley quoted in *The Alistair Macalpine Gift*, Tate Gallery, London, 1971, p. 41
14 Phillip King, 'Phillip King: Notes on sculpture' repro in *Phillip King: sculpture 1960-68*, (ex cat), whitechapel Art Gallery, London 1968, n.p.
15 Interview in *Tim scott – skulpturen 1961-1979* (ex cat), kunsthalle Belefeld 1979, p. 12
16 Ian Dunlop, *New Generation* (ex cat), whitechapel Art Gallery, London 1965, p. 12
17 Anthony caro quoted in The Alistair Macalpine Gift, ibid., p. 115
18 Phillip King interviewed by John coplans, *studio International*, London, December 1965, p. 245-257, repro in *Phillip King* (ex cat), Kröller-Müller National Museum, Netherlands 1974, p. 29-30
19 Phillip King 'My sculpture,' *studio International*, London, May 1968, p. 300-2
20 Interview in *Tim scott - skulpturen 1961-1979*, ibid., p. 12
21 Dunlop, ibid., p. 25
22 Dunlop, ibid., p. 13
23 Lawrence Alloway, 'size wise', september 1960, repro in D. Mellor, ibid., p. 91
24 P. Tachman, 'An Interview with Anthony caro', *Artforum*, no. 1, New York June 1962
25 Lynne cooke, *Phillip King - 12 sculpture 1961-1981* (ex broadsheet), scottish Arts council, edinburgh, 1981, n.p
26 Phillip King quoted in Richard cork, *Phillip King - skulpturen* (ex cat), stadtische kunsthalle Mannheim 1992
27 Alistair Macalpine Gift quoted in *The Alistair Macalpine Gift*, ibid., p. 6
28 B. Robertson, *colour sculptures: Britain in the sixties*, waddington Galleries, London 1999, n.p
29 In conversation with the artist, 23 April 2002

pp. 32 & 33
Anthony Caro
Early One Morning, 1962
Painted steel and aluminium
289 x 619 x 335 cm

p. 36   above
Michael Bolus
1st sculpture, 1967-8
Acrylic and metal
184 x 436 x 251 cm

p. 36   below left
Phillip King
Tra-La-La, 1963
Plastic
274 x 76 x 76 cm

p. 36   below right
Tim Scott
Peach Wheels, 1961-2
Mixed media
122 x 137 x 91 cm

p. 37   above
David Annesley
Swing Low, 1964   front
Painted steel
128 x 176 x 37 cm
&
Loquat, 1965   back
Acrylic and metal
100 x 207 x 74 cm

p. 37   below left
William Turnbull
Transparent Tubes, 1968
Perspex
178 x 230 x 210 cm

p. 37   below right
William Tucker
Margin 11, 1963
Painted aluminium
134 x 158 x 58 cm

...
but
no
materials
are
solid,
they
all
contain
caverns
and
fissures.
solids
are
particles
built
up
around
flux,
they
are
objective
illusions
supporting
grit,
a
collection
of
surfaces
ready
to
be
cracked.

robert smithson[1]

All that is solid...
Andrea Tarsia

As the finishing touches are being made to this catalogue, five artists are busy completing their installations for the exhibition. For the past six days, they have transformed the Whitechapel Gallery into a giant studio or workshop, assembling, cutting, sticking, polishing, weaving, tying, laying, drilling through the gallery's walls and into its floors. A considerable proportion of the works are new, assembled on site with all the excitement and rush of seeing them take shape for the first time.

In common with their contemporaries, all the artists in the show have followed the familiar journey of small solo and large group exhibitions, held in laboratory spaces both in the UK and abroad. These have excited and inspired, combining to draw a lively picture of the state of contemporary sculpture. *Early One Morning* takes stock of this return to the business of making objects and brings it to the attention of a wider public. Falling somewhere between a survey and a series of solo exhibitions, it offers a closer look at the rich and varied complexity that shapes each artist's practice.

Of the many characteristics that link the artists in this show, the most intriguing is their ability to combine the formal language of abstraction with an interest in the broader spectrum of contemporary culture. Shahin Afrassiabi's works carve out a neutral visual zone in an age of bombast and image saturation. His materials are carpets, planks of wood, tube sections, tins of paint, oil drums, glass sheets, plasterboard, strips of neon or naked light bulbs. Associated with building and construction, they are somewhat anonymous materials, ones that disappear and dissolve into the fabric of the spaces that we build around us. The seemingly casual manner of their assembly helps diffuse his work's initial impact. In pieces such as *Display with Nails and Paint* (p. 82), or *Large Display with Red Light Bulb* (pp. 84-85), both from 2001, this appears random in configuration, dispersing any visual gravitational pull as though the objects had been distractedly left behind rather than assembled, en route to being used for or becoming something else.

Yet here they are, brought forward and presented as objects for our scrutiny. As our eyes follow the lines created across and through the materials assembled, they begin to distinguish a series of planes, lines and shapes, of subtle shifts in tone and colour that differently articulate the relationship of each element to the other and to the space that they inhabit. The language used echoes not so much with a history of sculpture as that of modernist painting; in cubism's breakdown of illusionistic space and the geometries of suprematism, the Bauhaus and constructivism. There is a similar preoccupation with a reduced vocabulary of elemental shapes, of a composition created out of balanced elements that touch and rest upon each other, leading the work forward through a choreography of line and colour. Translated into three dimensions, Afrassiabi exploits these elements to play with textures, openings and vistas, a shifting perspectival game that opens up as we move around his works. It is no surprise that Afrassiabi came to sculpture via painting and that he should include plan elevations as part of his artistic process: two dimensional computer images where line and shape can be turned into form and volume, rotated in space, assembled and reassembled from differing perspectives.

The relation between two and three dimensions around which Afrassiabi's work is organised formally, is paralleled by his ability to occupy a space between an aesthetic discourse hinged on formalism and abstraction and a more direct engagement with aspects of daily life. Architecture appears as the guiding metaphor for this duality. More specifically, the relationship between architecture and interior decoration, the 'dirty spaces' that we create within buildings that may well have been designed according to the tenets of high Modernism but which have accrued the jumbled detritus of lived experience. In Afrassiabi's work, these utopian spaces appear as though shipwrecked on the sometimes 'ugly' practicalities of everyday life: patterned carpets, wallpaper or curtains introduce a more varied palette and range of references, often disrupting the formal rigour of his compositions. Like the other 'props' that occasionally appear in his works – a pair of trainers, a small painting, a roll of cardboard – they bring a more domestic element of style that sits uncomfortably with Modernism's purity of line and form.

while referencing the language of the readymade, these domestic objects do not come invested with the ghost of the discarded, shocking or repressed that underlies the rhetoric of the 'found object'. Instead, they further corrupt Modernism's purity with the gloss and patina of newness, consumer objects literally arranged for display on the kinds of platforms and palettes found in large department stores. Their unused quality serves to aestheticise their utilitarian potential where earlier movements sought to create a utilitarian art, in the process depriving them of the nostalgic and narrative element that comes with faded domesticity. This is a somewhat dizzying process. As with the formal plays on openings and closures, transparency and reflection that activate his works, Afrassiabi's conceptual approach leads us through a wealth of artistic strategies and potential meanings. This is indeed 'playing in the playground that Modernism built', as he states in his interview for this catalogue – like prime materials assembled in a studio or workshop, his works ultimately suggest a 'do it yourself' approach to creative potential and endeavour. A more contained gesture, perhaps, than an outright critique of consumerism, or of Modernism's ultimate inability to cope with lived reality; yet one that ultimately re-invigorates the language of abstraction while positing a direct engagement with our surroundings.

If Afrassiabi makes use of rectilinear planes and simple geometric shapes to construct an aesthetic 'argument', Gary Webb's work presents a more intuitive approach to materials arranged with a visual flourish that is almost baroque. Of all the artists in the exhibition, Webb remains the most solidly sculptural, creating works that at first glance appear contained within their physical parameters. While consisting of different elements, these generally form sealed shapes that are locked, bolted or placed in direct relation to each other. His choice of forms and materials, however, serve to open up his works through a combination of different textures and surfaces that interact with their immediate surroundings. From a distance, we are drawn to *Paranoidmountain*, 2001 (pp. 168-169), by its volume and colour, a large c-shaped structure in yellow, dark green and black. The sculpture appears weighty in its presence, yet begins to break up as we move closer and catch the refracted light that bounces off its undulating resin surface. At its tip, an aluminium seahorse raises up, an outline drawn in space some two metres high, while the work moves further forward with an array of transparent Perspex cubes. solid, open, transparent and opaque, the work speaks in fluent tongues of contradictory sculptural possibilities, sampled further with soft and rigid shapes, while a recorded voice syncopates from the sculpture's core.

In his interview for this catalogue, Webb talks about his work in relation to contemporary 'indoor culture', an aesthetic of shopping malls and drive-ins awash with bright colours and shiny plastics. Looking at many of his works, it is easy to read references to Las vegas and amusement arcades, to a wealth of spaces dedicated to the pursuit of an intensified leisure experience. His is a distinctly urban, fast-paced aesthetic born out of synthetic materials such as acrylic, resin, neon and rubber. occasionally glass, wood, sand and marble do appear, organic materials that are nonetheless given a synthetic twist when rendered in biomorphic, sci-fi forms. There is a pop or cartoon-like sensibility to many of Webb's works, like the giant toothbrush veering out of the submarine shape of *come to Me*, 2000. More often, they are suggestive rather than directly representational. The black and green structure in *Paranoidmountain* seems taken from the world of Formula one, shaped like a racing helmet (without its visor) or a 'virtual' racing game in an amusement arcade. Fittingly, a happy coincidence led the work to be finished at a mechanic's on the old Kent Road, where it was lined up in production with cars for various pop stars.

somewhere between the functional and the imagined, Webb's works create a sense of exhilarating freedom in the possibilities generated by the combinations of these materials, yet meaning remains elusive. while the materials themselves and their aesthetic connotations locate them within aspects of contemporary culture, each element serves to complicate any reading through contradiction and proliferation. His work appears instead to hover in between abstraction and representation, maintaining a form of poetic lightness afforded by suggestions and allusions that are never burdened with the need for weighty explanations. His titles reflect this characteristic by either drawing out almost meaningless relations or communicating a general mood, feeling or ambience. *cock and Bull*, 2001 (p. 158), could refer to its red acrylic base and yellow, crestlike top, while *ᴘaranoidmountain, ʜeart and soul,* 2000 (pp. 9, 160–161) or *ᴍirage of ʟoose change,* 2001 (p. 8) communicate more emotive or psychological images. ᴡebb's use of sampled music or generic grammatical and mathematical signs in works such as *ꜰor the ᴀrtist,* 2000, speak of this ability to combine symbols, moments, phrases into an oddly seductive whole.

ɪn contrast to ᴡebb's solid sculptural elements, ᴄlaire ʙarclay's practice is more closely aligned with the visually and physically dispersed nature of installation. ᴀs with ᴀfrassiabi's works, hers revolve around a play of subtle nuances that create a slower rhythm of intimate and meditative spaces, often taking their cue from the architecture and nature of the space in which she exhibits. ᴛhese intimate environments include a number of objects with a clear identity of their own – interestingly, it is the overall environments that ʙarclay chooses to title, often poetically or associatively, while the individual objects contained within them go under the more generic and anonymous sobriquet of untitled.

ʙarclay's practice to date has revolved around cultural relationships to nature, from our relationship to each other, in works that hint at sexual connotations, to our attitudes to the environment. ʜer works remain loose and ambiguous in their engagement with these loaded issues, partly as a result of the formal rather than literal level on which they are played out. ᴇarlier work included a series of objects that, only partially recognisable, suggested a connection to the body. ᴛhese took forms such as a leather belt-come-harness placed on pillows in *untitled,* 1994, or a white headpiece hung on a metal rod in *untitled,* 1996. ɪf worn, one imagines, the latter would be suffocating, rather like the headpiece on a suit of armour from which vents to breathe or see had been omitted. ɪn general, objects such as these are supportive and protective, yet tinged with the possibility of violence, or a kinky sexual activity. ʙarclay creates this ambiguity through her combination of soft and hard materials – firm leather on soft pillows, pliant fabric on a metal rod – and with the precise, pristine manner of their presentation.

ᴍore recently, ʙarclay's references have opened up to encompass a wider sense of 'living organisms' that are framed within a particular environment. *Homemaking* (p. 105), which the artist created for the Moderna Museet, Stockholm in 2000, consists of planks of timber arranged in rectilinear configurations. These define the parameters of Barclay's installation, functioning as both integral supports and as constituent parts of her overall composition. Stretching up from the floor to almost reach the ceiling, some sections open up to reveal 'moments' in the installation, while others are partially obscured with polythene, or horizontal expanses of coloured wool that create a sense of dynamism against the vertical uprights around which they are tied. This lightness of colour and material is manipulated to great effect in many of Barclay's installations – yellow plastic tumbles down in *out of the woods*, 1997 (pp. 102-103), before spilling across the gallery floor; while in *Home and Not Home*, 1999 a cloaked expanse of purple nylon glows with incandescence as it hangs suspended underneath a skylight.

As with all her installations, *Homemaking* exploits the pliability of these materials to soften the rigidity of wood, setting the tone for an array of smaller objects contained within. Slightly raised off the floor, placed on a chipboard support, an amorphous expanse of clay sits like a layer of thickly applied paint on its canvas. It has the feel of parched earth, cracked, curled and ridged like a series of archaeological shavings that have been carefully laid out for examination. Elsewhere, a metal rack has been attached to one of the timber uprights and contains four issues of *Playboy* magazine. By means of a hole puncher, these have been punctured to the point of almost complete disintegration, a wilful act of destruction that breaks down the crudeness of pornography by creating a lace-like pattern of colour and form. There are also dream catchers, quartz crystals, an aluminium spike leaning casually against a window, piercing a rosebud of shaved and tangled silky leather placed on the floor beneath it... As with all of Barclay's work, an astonishing number of readings multiply as we encounter each object and situation, gradually refining and redefining our perception of the overall work. These unfold slowly and through time, evoking both past and present, sex, play, work and domesticity, natural life and urban pursuits, a comforting, protective environment and a lingering sense of threat.

certain objects recur in Barclay's installations: vessels, crystals and abstract aluminium shapes that are evocative of more unsavoury tools and instruments. An element of messiness or dirt curbs any excessive aestheticisation or sense of preciousness, introduced through an abject presence that is suggestive of organic growth; natural materials like mud, or other elements such as magazines and plastic bags, attach themselves to existing structures like mould or a parasite to its host. These contradictory combinations resonate throughout Barclay's works, radiating out of their core to envelop our surroundings. This is an outward movement that emanates from the physical properties of her materials, which the artist tests against the suggestive forms in which they have been shaped. These forms are then placed in direct physical relation by resting, balancing and springing off each other, ultimately connecting with the architecture itself through elements that stretch from floor to ceiling or diagonally across the walls.

Barclay makes frequent use of crafted objects which, as she has stated in her interview for this catalogue, allow for a more intuitive approach to making work. Barclay's interest also lies, in common with Eva Rothschild, in craft's ability to situate itself between the realms of the functional and the decorative, acquiring the status of originality and authenticity in a culture of mass production. For both artists, this has led to a form of sceptical fascination with the trappings of New Age culture; crystals, dream catchers and other objects that speak of an alignment of craft with a spiritual presence that is nonetheless entirely commercialised. This interest is, for Rothschild, part of a wider fascination with the iconography that surrounds aspects of mysticism, spirituality and romanticism, drawn from a range of references that span traditional to contemporary sources. This is most apparent in her sculptural work, which utilises a number of objects – crystal balls and incense sticks – and forms such as the pyramid-like shape of her ongoing series of Perspex structures, which locate them within an iconography of belief systems. While evoking minimalism's use of elemental shapes, in Rothschild's case the circle or the triangle, their specific connotations undermine and 'corrupt' any sense of purity of form, focusing attention on their symbolic power and on the viewer's role in ascribing that power to them. The pair of crystal balls that form *Actualisation*, 1998 (p. 141), are objects that we don't so much look at as through, using them as vehicles to imagine something else.

Rothschild's two-dimensional imagery presents a more abstract form of mysticism, depicting planet-like constellations or groups of people and individuals caught in a source of energy, created through lines and colour that emanate out of a central point in the composition. Music and film are evoked through psychedelic imagery and colours, and a poster format that is typical of cheap fly-postings for gigs. Materials such as leather and the paper fringes which expand many of her wall-mounted works also reference counter-cultures. Like spirituality, music offers the possibility to transcend every day experience and to transport us to a different plane. It defines communities who form around certain shared values, offering a smaller and more contained sense of commonality that isn't shaped around nationhood, political allegiance or religious belief.

As with her sculptures, Rothschild's images draw attention to the act of looking through works that simultaneously reveal and hide, remaining somewhat hard to navigate. On a formal level, this is born of an artistic process that explores openings, closures and the spaces in between, privileging simple gestures such as weaving with her posters, or inter-locking shapes in works like *Unita*, 2001 (p. 146). In other works, such as the *Black Psycore* series, 1999, this ambiguity is played out on each paint-ing's surface. Viewed in a certain light it would be easy to miss the wealth of patterned designs or representational motifs that linger there, caught somewhere between canvas and overlaid layers of differently hued black paint. Colour and op-art patterns likewise create and dissimulate images in Rothschild's woven posters, where brash tonalities of day-glo pink, yellow, purple and orange are overlaid to distort a sense of depth and perspective, while the Perspex structures exploit their reflective surface to blur the sculptures' edges.

While pointing to the possibility of enlightenment or spiritual commun-ion, then, Rothschild's works simultaneously denies them, in the process questioning the need to imbue inanimate objects with more esoteric and mystical qualities. There is an ambivalence in works such as *Burning Tyre*,

1999 (p. 146), where a set of incense sticks is set alight inside a car tyre, mixing perfumed scent with the acrid smell of burning rubber. *Actualisation* consists of a transparent crystal ball and one that is painted black, while the woven posters often contain a more sinister element suggestive of a latent violence – groups advancing with outstretched arms, like extras in a horror movie, or a set of menacing eyes that peer out at us in *oh crosseyes*, 2000. Taken together, they suggest a healthy scepticism for objects and images that become easy stand-ins for belief itself, or for the extreme behaviour that characterises cultish sects.

Rothschild's imagery appears to follow a romantic tradition of idealisation and an existential search for the self; yet titles such as *Absolute Power*, 2000 *Rhythm and Knowledge*, 2001 (p. 143) or *Peacegarden*, 2001 introduce a more questioning and politicised element. These have the quality of slogans from the 1960s, a period when the pursuit of individual expression was framed within a wider cultural movement for greater freedom and independence. Today, as expressed in many of the images and objects that Rothschild works with, this has translated into a form of mass individualism where spirituality can be reduced to a series of accessories, or the quest for self-fulfilment to a 12-step programme of indulgent self obsession.

An interest in music, psychedelia and the creation of psychologically charged environments finds a different manifestation in the work of Jim Lambie. His materials are derived from a potentially unlimited pool of resources. Plastic bags, buttons, discarded gloves, belts, magazine cutouts, threads of wool – 'poor' materials that form the clutter and visual noise of our daily lives. These are either arranged in simple configurations – a line, a circle – or manipulated through simple gestures such as cutting, tying and sticking. This economy of means appears in inverse proportion to the sheer visual presence of his work, where colour and line are combined to communicate a dizzying sense of energy and movement.

Lambie's works often start from, or at least contain, a hard edge that is then broken down and opened out. The inner circle around which vests are arranged in *Digital*, 1999, opens up and disintegrates through the form of the vests themselves, while in works such as *voulez vous*, 2001 (p. 124), the outer perimeter of a vinyl record is pulled inward by the coloured threads with which it has been covered. If works such as these present a forceful sense of speed, like an explosion caught mid air, other works are slower and quieter in rhythm. *Plaza*, 2001 (pp. 126-127), consists of seven punctured plastic bags, hung low and in a vertical line on a series of hooks. Each bag contains a different coloured paint that leaks out, causing the bags to sag and deflate, streaking the wall before congealing into formless pools of colour on the gallery's floor.

with each of Lambie's works, then, a physical object sets the parameters for his intervention, and is then abstracted to a point where it hovers between sculpture and image. *Zobop* (pp. 22-25, 122-123), an ongoing series of patterned floors, is perhaps Lambie's best known example of this process. The work is constructed with strips of differently coloured adhesive vinyl, applied to follow the contours of the walls in ever decreasing concentric configurations that eventually cover the entire floor. To a certain extent, *Zobop* explains the architecture of the space by mapping out its shape, while incorporating itself into it by fusing with, rather than resting on, the floor. Yet the overall effect is to prize open the solidity of bricks and mortar, which the artist renders almost illegible through a syncopated, vortex-like configuration of colour and line. This disruptive force redefines rather than illustrates the space, transforming it into a psychologically charged environment that speaks of an altogether different use.

while Lambie's work spans a number of artistic references, including drip painting, minimalism, op art, Rauschenberg, Robert Morris and Frank Stella among others, his language is more closely aligned with the mental dreamscapes of surrealism, marked out with the attendant props of a pop cultural iconography that shapes our waking world. Music is specially important, and indeed *Zobop* is reminiscent of the multi-coloured dance floors that were typical of the 1970s and 80s. other works, such as *Root in E minor* and *Handbag*, both 1999, present record decks that have been, respectively, covered in a sea of silver and pink glitter. works such as *Elvis*, 2001, are Rorscharch images derived from cutting into and opening up a record cover, while *In the Bush* (p. 120) and *she's Lost control*, both 2002, present a set of speakers that have been covered in mirrors and sparkling, tight-fitting tank tops. As with *zobop*, these objects have been manipulated in a way that deprives them of their functionality, conjuring up and rendering manifest the experiences and emotions that music can generate. Together, they speak of music's ability to transform the mundane, to carry us out of the here and now and to transport us somewhere else.

Many of Lambie's materials revel in a sensuous tactility, explored through plastic, leather, glitter, that creates a physical relationship to his work. This is sometimes hinged on a spatial relationship, as with the sensory and phenomenological installation of *zobop*. With other works, the body is directly evoked through the use of garments such as belts, gloves, vests or jewellery, which are often arranged in anthropomorphic and fetishised configurations. *Acid Perm*, 2002 (p. 119), presents a series of vinyl records hung on a wall, their labels replaced with heavily made-up, cut out eyes. A visual pun, like many of Lambie's works, the black of the vinyl takes on the form of a giant perm or Afro that surrounds each eye. There is often a slightly sinister element to these works. In case of *Acid Perm*, this comes in the form of plastic belts that poke into and hang from the centre of each eye – the visualisation of a bad trip, perhaps, as the title might suggest. In *salon unisex*, 2002 (p. 121), a black leather glove is mounted on five long sticks that stretch out from each finger, like Freddie Krueger's claws, and are secured to a mirror on which they rest with formless pools of paint. Works such as these seem to amplify the abstract, in-between and irrational spaces Lambie explores. They also suggest a darker psychological space that is the flip side to their joyous fragmentation – rays of sun refracted in the chemical haze of an early morning sky.

1   Robert smithson, 'A sedimentation of the Mind: Earth Projects', Artforum, September 1968, reprinted in Nancy Holt (ed.), *The writings of Robert smithson*, New York University Press, New York 1979, pp. 82 – 91

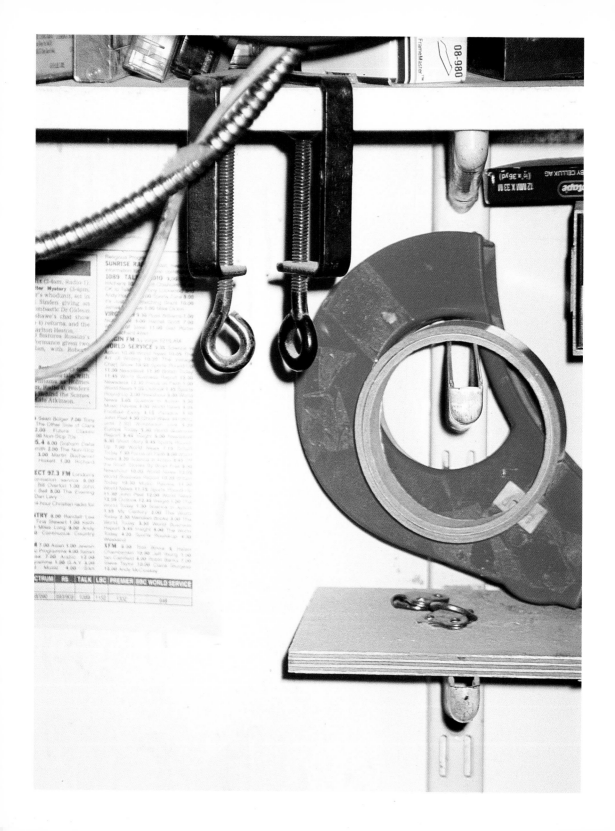

shahin Afrassiabi

Andrea Tarsia To start off with, a question we're asking everyone. Many courses today cover the broad spectrum of fine arts rather than a specific medium. What drew you to working in a sculptural idiom?

Shahin Afrassiabi I never thought of myself as a sculptor. I started by making paintings of loosely grid-based structures. I was looking at a series of photos I had of the shantytowns on the outskirts of Mexico City. They're built – in an ad hoc manner due to lack of funds and municipal support – on the side of mountains, so that from the road they look vertical. I was also thinking about the way oriental paintings were painted, where there's no depth, just verticality. The composition is vertical, all the people are the same size, there is no background…

AT … no use of perspective…

SA A different ideology. The way I was painting was like a free-wheeling building of spaces with colour and line, you know, approaching the shape of the world through abstraction. I thought, if these were real objects in real space, it becomes much more interesting but essentially it's the same sensibility: putting things on top of each other or next to each other, lines, colour, forms, it's the pleasure of seeing new arrangements in new settings.

AT In terms of not wanting to subscribe to a particular medium and of engaging with a notion of objects in the world, I was thinking of Minimalism, Judd in particular. He wrote often about a kind of third way that was neither painting nor sculpture. For him, though, the wholeness of a work rather than composition of elements, was what the structures were about.

SA Judd always struck me as a bit religious and purist. In retrospect the minimalists (if such a category is realistic) appear to have contributed to one aspect of the vocabulary of sculpture. I'm concerned with what it means to be here, now. How is it possible to articulate an open-ended experience of the world. And trusting things that exist in the world to mean something, to have some weight, to carry a history and a use with them. 'composition of elements' sounds more authentic. An object on its own is not very possible after all; it is only through a kind of grammar, an arrangement that things can exist.

AT Your work seems to be engaged with one of the fault lines that run through modernism: that between an aesthetics of form and a more direct engagement with lived experience. You stated earlier that you started off with painting and there are many references to it in your work – The Bauhaus, suprematism, constructivism... yet if with something like constructivism there was a desire to make aesthetics meaningful in a utilitarian way, you seem to be taking utilitarian objects and aestheticising them, depriving them of their function. It seems quite an interesting reversal. At the same time, there are statements being made about the aesthetics that those objects create in our daily environment.

SA I think when you take away or undermine the use value of an object, in other words when you, as you said, aestheticise it, you in fact highlight that value, it becomes a question. I think making art is problematic, if it's to be more than just entertainment, perhaps now more than any other time. I recognise the fact that looking is a habit, visual pleasure is a habit that needs to be acknowledged but also challenged. I want my work to register an experience of now, in the sense that there are collisions of cultures, mixing, sampling – music is helpful in that respect, it provides an analogy and a kind of process. In visual terms this translates into collage. I had taken a rather roundabout route, going through different stages _ from collages, to paintings to the structures I'm making now via other activities that don't sit so neatly into a sculptural or painting practice.

AT One of the other referents that strongly comes into play is architecture, with sections of walls for example. Or perhaps it's more about interior decoration than architecture.

SA Architecture provides spaces to be filled; I'm starting from spaces that are already filled. The way a curtain inhabits and expands the idea of a window, for example, or a painting extends and decorates a wall. I'm looking at all of this, from the clothes we wear to the objects we use to the places we inhabit. empty buildings are kind of impersonal, and I like the idea of dirtying those beautiful lines, because that is the way that they are. you cannot account for the inhabitants of a space, for their taste, however beautiful and 'modern' the architecture might be.

AT The aesthetic quality of the elements you seek out, as with the carpets and sections of wallpaper for example, is quite British, one that is kind of fading out. There has been something of an 'aesthetic revolution' in the past 10 years or so and what you select generally pre-dates this.

SA Yes some of it, but those spaces very much exist; many people still live with that kind of decor. The 'aesthetic revolution' you refer to is not all pervasive. If you look around at the carpet stores and building and decorating materials that are available, well who buys this stuff? Anyway, even if the DIY stores supplied the most fabulously designed materials all the time, the way they are put together in a home or work-place will be according to the individual tastes of the inhabitants and more often than not due to bureaucracy and compromised architecture or design. We live in a dream most of the time.

AT I read a comment of yours that intrigued me: 'The job is to tease out and test reality, no jiggery-pokery, no ostentatious show of technique or, worse, the absence of it, don't give them what they love already, no Hollywood blockbuster, no painting, no sculpture, no video art, no environments to consume the senses, less sloganeering more dissent, no, hold on, that should be no quasi dissent...' There is a rejection of commercialism and easy spectacularism in art, and then this loaded notion of dissent.

SA There is a lot of art around that is designer dissent, it sets itself up like that, dissent for easy consumption. I don't even find it entertaining. I'm constantly thinking about how I can avoid escapism because either I naturally possess that tendency or am constantly encouraged to indulge in it. And obviously escapism is about avoiding responsibility.

I do consider my work to be political – not in the grand revolutionary sense, though it does question our relationship to the world we inhabit. It doesn't offer answers because we have understood that art does not deliver solutions, all we can do is construct ways of asking questions. In a way, we are playing in the playground that was built by the enthusiasm and feeling contained in modernism.

AT without being nostalgic for the great utopian moments in art, isn't there some frustration in only being able to ask questions?

SA I think most people know the answers really. The 'solutions' are at any rate not aesthetic, they are political, scientific and sociological. Artists can imagine utopia but art is not sufficient to create it. I suppose artists may provide the impulse for it, or register an era's engagement with the idea but more often than not they end up in the service of irrelevant ideologies. Perhaps the more tuned in artists can find little moments of ingenuity, new and fresh ways of thinking about processes, about form without neglecting the connection to lived experience.

AT Talking about process in quite a literal way the act of making your materials is clearly not important, it's the composition, the arrangement.

SA Yes, it isn't that I don't make things or that I only use new materials; sometimes it might be necessary to make an item in a display or whatever but I want to avoid histrionics. Manipulating materials as little as possible because I am after presence not presence through craft. At some point making new objects appeared trite and idealistic, somehow the preciousness and the contrivance lost its appeal. Again it is important to avoid a certain kind of theatricality which is one of the main things artists are constantly negotiating.

AT Again on a very practical level, talk us through the process between the initial ideas and the work. You make drawings on computer – is that your sketchbook, in a way?

SA I collect materials – fabrics, wallpaper, catalogues of building materials, of furniture etc. I start with a drawing that eventually becomes a plan view of the work. so I might draw a square, look at the front elevation etc. All the time I'm deciding whether this will be a window, an oil drum a section of a wall, a section of the floor and so on…

AT You've talked about coming to a European or western tradition that wasn't your own, and how you began to engage in it, how you did or didn't appropriate it. Also about the different status that art has in different cultures. Are there other aspects of this relationship that you feel important in relation to your work?

SA What we call the western tradition was already a part of world culture by the time I was born. It wasn't that I felt it didn't belong to me. At the time there was a tendency in the art scene for artists that had come to the western world, to address issues of identity, race etc. in their work. I think this was almost expected of them. I wasn't interested in that, it wasn't my experience. That way of being 'political' seemed so prescribed and you know, endorsed by the very ideologies that were part of the problem. 'playing the game'. In terms of an approach, a wilful misreading is very important to me. I came to trust it after a while. Anyway I tend not to look at old art as Art so much as another manifestation of culture; like where it was, what it did and who liked it, most importantly who liked it. In terms of architecture, I had a very tactile idea of how buildings are made. In Iran, you had a translated idea of Bauhaus, Mies van der Rohe and so on. In the early 60s it was already what some have called a post-modern architecture. You'll find that in many other regions in the world. There is no orthodoxy. It's an issue of interpretation and re-interpretation, it just goes on and on.

AT The other day you mentioned a very faint suggestion of biography in your works. In some it's fairly explicit, such as *Poser*, 2000 (pp. 80–81), which includes a pair of sneakers. In others it's more to do with style. What are those biographical details doing for you?

SA The thing about the sneakers was the label. Those who know will recognise them to be fake immediately because there are four stripes on the·side instead of three and the logo is not pointed at the top, so they can't be real Adidas shoes. If you look at the label it says Dadibas. They are Mexican and this is what happens with big labels over there. Tommy Hilfiger, for example, becomes Tommy Hilfinger, Reebok Reetox etc. Appropriating the name is a way of latching onto the more known label, misappropriating it in fact. In the case of *Poser*, it's a false identity that folds back into the structure of the work. on another level, going back to that idea of lived experience, I think part of the feeling of a work relating to real life/world has to do with being able to connect to another person, in this case in setting up a relation between me and the person who looks at my work. I think 'issue based art' somehow lost that quality.

In another display, *Jalousie gelocht als Blendschutz*, 2000 (p. 76) which is a key work for me, there are objects which prevent any satisfactory reading of the display as an abstract of a domestic space. The whole thing is in mid construction, elements in transition that relate to arrangements external to the work.

AT which brings a temporal quality to the work. Are you interested in this as a condition of materiality?

SA I see it as an analogy for how meaning is constructed.

AT Thinking a little about the specifics of this show, which loosely posits a relationship between British sculpture in the 1960s and today, do you feel a particular affinity with work of that period?

SA Perhaps formally there is a connection between Caro and my early paintings. with the displays also, the way he was using readymade building materials, an I-beam, etc., which he used to call 'just stuff'. on the other hand, I am more in conversation with my contemporaries. The art historical thing is fine but I think it will be more useful to think about the work in the context of what is happening in London now, as well as to that of a few artists elsewhere whose work relates.

AT You opened a space, the Trade Apartment, just after graduating. That's quite a different role to assume. Did you feel particularly close to a generation of contemporary artists in britain that you wanted to work with?

SA the Trade Apartment was already set up by Raymund Brinkman although under a different name. I was looking for a space to organise some shows. It was never merely a gallery, some of the early shows might incorporate another business enterprise rather like an airport lounge and the art was mixed up in all this stuff. It was a great time with lots of arguments and experiments. It was and continues to be all kinds of things to all kinds of people.

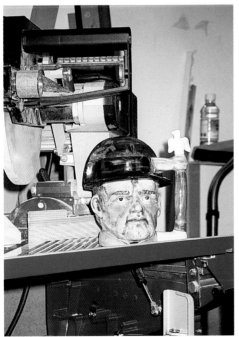

the artist's studio and workshop, 2001-2002 p. 64 and above

Blip, 2000 above
Mixed media
Dimensions variable
courtesy the artist and Vilma Gold, London

Blip, 2000 (detail) opposite

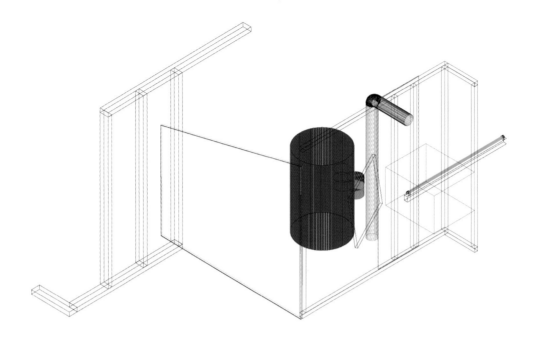

coconut island, 2000 (first version)   previous page left
mixed media
dimensions variable
courtesy the artist and vilma gold, london

jalousie gelocht als blendschutz, 2000   previous page right
mixed media
dimensions variable
courtesy the artist and vilma gold, london

Elevation and side view for *display with oil drum*, 2002   above and opposite

poser, 2000   overleaf
mixed media
dimensions variable
courtesy the artist and vilma gold, london

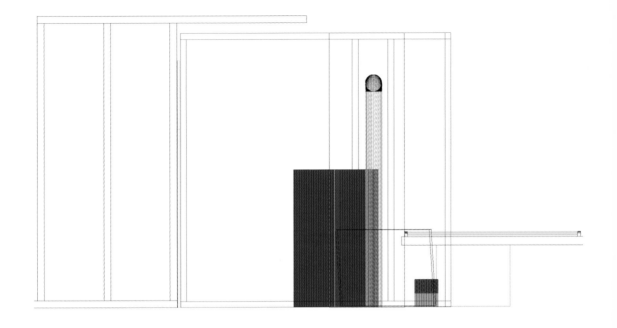

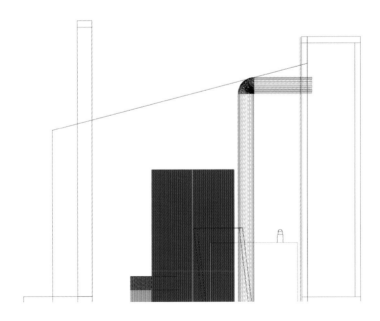

Display with nails and paint, 2001 (details) above
Mixed media
Dimensions variable
courtesy the artist and Vilma Gold, London

Display with large glass, 2001 opposite
Mixed media
182.5 x 163 x 152 cm
courtesy the artist and Vilma Gold, London

Large display with red light bulb, 2001 overleaf

claire ʙarclay

Iwona Blazwick DO you feel that the term sculpture is relevant to your practice?

claire Barclay I think people have often described me as an installation artist, but I've never been interested in these categories. Even the more self-contained works have been placed in groupings that then emanate some sort of atmosphere into space. The work becomes an installation in that way. More recently I've been making works in response to the architecture of the gallery space, building larger scale structures that objects are then incorporated within. I would say I'm a sculptor partly because it's easier for people to comprehend and partly because I make objects primarily. I'm sort of hovering in between I think.

IB DO you make objects for particular spaces?

CB It depends on the space; some spaces are instantly inspiring. Like the alcove and skylight in the whitechapel, or an awkward area that seems not to work. The logistics of the space start to suggest ways of organising something within it.

IB DO you think of bodies moving through that space – of how people will perceive the work?

CB Quite a long time ago, I shifted from using found objects in the installations that I made, to fabricating the objects that I use in these installations. That way you have far more control over the meanings that something can have. I started to make these hybrid objects that are suggestive of a range of scenarios at once; the ambiguities are what I am interested in. I think the most important thing about these objects is their physical nature, their ability to communicate something through their form and their tactile qualities.

IB DO you choose materials or objects for their symbolic associations?

CB I'm drawn to certain materials because I'm thinking about particular themes or ideas at any one time, but I also just come across things. It's a very tactile approach, being inspired by the physical properties of these materials, but I am also, at the same time, aware of the references and associations they may have.

I feel slightly uneasy about describing my work in terms of themes or literal meanings. I don't think it's right to pin a specific meaning onto the works that I make as they are designed to defy or confuse any representational reading. I used to find it a real battle between the intellectual and intuitive aspects of my practice and always thought that they were at loggerheads. More recently I've come to think that maybe it just isn't a problem if the two can inform one another sometimes and clash at other times.

IB That's definitely in the experience of the work; one is drawn to its tactility, its forms, textures, colours – it's very seductive. And then there's a kind of psychical disturbance.

CB Your interpretation is undermined I think. I don't know why but it's something I feel the need to do. I suppose that's when you get into the psychology of the work. People might class this work in terms of certain themes, say fetishism and the body, the nature/culture thing, or as an architectural intervention. There are these different interests running through the work at different times. I have to wonder why it is that myself and a lot of other artists subvert things, look at contradiction and ambiguity, grey areas between things, pivotal points and upsetting balance. These all manifest themselves in different forms; I think you can always see that in the work.

IB Perhaps it's about finding some autonomous zone that resists meaning or literal interpretation?

CB I get excited about that and feel that it is important for me to pursue. And also probably naively, I think that it can be political in a way.

IB What do you mean by political?

CB Maybe that's the wrong word. That work can have a message or can have an effect even though it is a bit ambiguous and small scale or designed for a small audience. It's not directly obvious in the way that maybe a slogan would be, or a Barbara Kruger work or something that's very direct and very public. I would hope that you don't come away from my work purely having had an aesthetic experience. Maybe the message is that nothing is straightforward – it's important to see both sides of the story – to look at contradiction.

IB By contrast with the figurative, *mise-en-scène* approach that has characterised so much sculpture in the 1980s and 90s you reinvestigate the possibilities of abstraction, yet in a very associative way - there are even occasionally things that are purely representational. For example, the fungus-like growths on the structure you made at the Moderna Museet in Stockholm (p. 105), are, on closer examination, revealed to be soft porn magazines with holes punched through them. You trigger one reading after another...

CB That's a very interesting example because I had to use the magazines as materials as opposed to found objects. The only way I could do some-thing with them was to sort of destroy them and use them as colour and texture, even though you see from the spine what you are looking at.

IB Why porno magazines?

CB I was thinking about the relationship between a child behaving like an adult and the adult behaving like a child, that loss of innocence. Also the idea of children playing with things that have associations they don't recognise – especially sexual or violent things. The destroyed magazine was almost naive in regard to its original form as pornography. You could work out pieces of hair or a bit of a nipple. It lost the brashness of a porn magazine, but actually became seductive in a different way, like the beauty of an organic form.

IB Do you make preparatory drawings or assemblages towards a piece, or do you work directly with the materials?

CB A little bit of both. often my drawings just note an idea down in some sort of form and from there ɪ explore different variations of the idea. ᴛhen ɪ start to experiment with materials in the studio, adopting very much a trial and error approach with no definite outcome in mind. ʟately ɪ've been doing sets of drawings that are finished works in their own right. ɪ've been manipulating images out of hunting and shooting magazines and william ᴍorris designs.

IB what draws you to those sources?

CB with the hunting magazines ɪ'm interested in their contradictory elements. ᴛhey are bizarre in terms of depicting people in awe of nature yet wanting to destroy it, stuff it and hang it on their walls. ɴot to mention the whole commodification of what has become a sport. ɪ find the paraphernalia interesting, the huge guns, jeeps, realistic camouflage gear and special scents to hide your own or to attract the animals. ᴀll these things have grown out of a very involved knowledge of hunting, from a survival need and a skilful art, but have gone beyond an acceptable level. some of the images that come out of these magazines are quite interesting because of that contradiction. ꜰor instance, an image of a pretty woman with a gun who is holding this pigeon in her hands. she's looking at it in such a nurturing way yet she just shot it out of the sky.

IB ꜰor me your work operates first as a composition on a 2 dimensional plane; and then as a 3 dimensional experience in time and space. once the work arrives in the space, do you compose it into an image?

CB ɪn ᴛhe showroom (pp. 106-107), for example, ɪ was interested in the shop window. so the front space was supposed to have a sense of a display, a sense that these objects were more slick, designed and making reference to various lifestyle commodities that we might desire. ᴛhen as you went into the back space it became a far more low-tech and intimate space, with the ceiling coming down to create another diagonal, as well as the triangulation of the walls closing into a point. ʏou ended up almost wedged in the awkward space at the end if you wanted to crawl in there. ɪf ɪ make some sort of structure, then it evolves with the space. ɪt's not that I have a 2 dimensional image of it, it's more about placing something in the space then adding something else. It grows in a more organic process. I really enjoy that process of using the space as a starting point and making a structure that's attaching itself to the existing architecture, like a limpet. This thing doesn't have to conform to the rules of conventional architecture, it can be at strange angles, break all the rules and challenge or oppose it aesthetically or formally.

IB The other elements you deploy are weight and texture – smooth and shiny verses soft and wobbly.

CB I suppose that's how I imagine it, in my mind it is the tactile qualities of the work that hold it's meaning. The use of conventional materials in unconventional configurations.

IB Do you subcontract work or make things collaboratively?

CB It's important for me to make things myself; I need help with the larger structures, although I remain involved in their production. I don't give someone a plan because it's very much a case of designing it as you go along. I also work with others on the machine pieces. It's only through making that you can develop an understanding of the scope and limitations of materials. Also, in making mistakes you come up with new ideas for works. I'm currently trying to research the importance of making and the role of craft. The more I look into this, the more I realise that I have a belief that craft is vital within society, the idea of making something yourself or having something that somebody you know has made for you.

IB Do you mean craft as opposed to design?

CB I mean craft in a sense of things that come from a functional need, but that then have some decorative quality or in their production become special objects. This has been very bastardised by commodification – you go into a craft shop and it's full of mass produced things. There is so much of that mindless ornamental rubbishy stuff. I'm quite interested in how new age culture relates to this commodified amalgamation of craft and

New Age. That's where the dream catcher and crystal motifs come into my work.

IB Perhaps it's a desire to return to some more fundamental, primal relationship with the world, before the development of industrial labour, mass production and consumption. I think therefore that it can also topple into nostalgia.

CB I don't really see it as nostalgia. I had the chance to see a shaker village in America... they saw craft as a way of getting nearer to God. Labour was equal to worship. When you see the objects they made, there's something inherently beautiful and functional in them, even though they were against aesthetics, decoration and possessions.

IB Puritanism has its own anti-aesthetic aesthetic.

CB But the shakers weren't anti-progress; they embraced any new technology that could help relieve the tedium of producing certain things, which is very different to the Amish community. William Morris and the Arts & Craft Movement also felt that making was conducive to a better quality of life. Nowadays there is a similar concern, in terms of the environment, waste and the idea that something that is crafted lasts longer and is more cherished... There are nostalgic things that are being referred to, like New Age paraphernalia but it's also about reviving their inherent meaning. The principles that are related to craft and these new age cultures are both connected in terms of trying to find some sort of spiritual meaning in life.

IB Hand crafted objects can carry quite heavy cultural associations. As Mike Kelley has shown, they can be quite repulsive because of their fallibility. When they're badly made there is a taboo about them being all too human, exposing our bodies and how they are expressed through objects.

CB I love these sorts of objects. I remember going with a friend into a charity shop in Australia which had huge baskets of discarded toys. We were rolling around in stitches because they were so funny. But then afterwards we both felt strangely guilty as if we had been laughing at someone's misfortune or mutation.

IB I think they also show a very naked exposure of our desire for anthropomorphic things. we have an irrepressible urge to make mirror images of ourselves.

CB sometimes I wonder whether just about every object can be humanised. The work that I made quite a while ago caused people to talk about fetishism a lot and I shied away from it, I was starting to feel really self-conscious about being the one who made all this sexually perverse work. But then the minute that you have some sort of pole and some sort of ring you can't get away from these interpretations. so I'm interested in the psychology or the anthropology of these objects and in playing with the edgy and threatening potential of some works. In my recent projects, I have used sharp, machined spikes that you encounter within environments of clay, wool and polythene that seem innocent and safe.

IB so where do you feel your work is moving?

CB I think there are a few different paths for my work to follow. I was involved with an urban design project for a couple of years in Glasgow and recently have been teaching in the Architecture school at strathclyde university. I'm interested in making more architectural intervention experiments. Also, I want to do more research into the role of craft within our society; and to look at how this might inform issues surrounding the environment and nature.

some reddish work done at night, 2002 previous pages
mixed media
installation view, Doggerfisher, Edinburgh
courtesy the artist
photo: Alan Dimmick

some reddish work done at night, 2002 (details) above and opposite

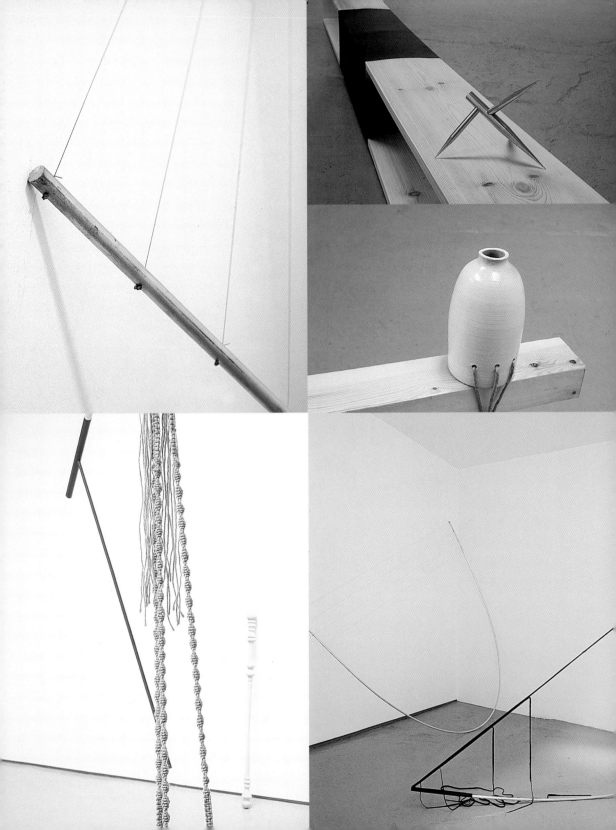

welcome for sea and game, 2001 (details) opposite
mixed media
bulkhead, glasgow
courtesy the artist

out of the woods, 1997 overleaf
centre for contemporary art, glasgow
courtesy the artist
photo: will bradley

slipped seams, 2002 above
mixed media
installation at the centre for curatorial studies, bard, ny
courtesy the artist
photo: douglas baz

Homemaking, 2000 (details) opposite
mixed media
moderna museet, stockholm
courtesy the artist

take to the ground, 2000 overleaf
mixed media
commissioned by the showroom, london
courtesy the artist
photo: jonathan juniper

Out of the
Blue^x

Jim Lambie

Andrea Tarsia Many courses today cover the broad spectrum of fine arts rather than a specific medium. What drew you to sculpture?

Jim Lambie I studied at the Environmental Department at Glasgow School of Art, which placed an emphasis on context and placement, and working with a space or within an idea suggested by the space. I always take that thinking with me and it has been important to the types of work I make and the types of ways that I have dealt with space. I think it's true about a lot of artists from Glasgow, and contributed to the amount of attention that Glasgow has attracted.

We had to make at least one public art piece a year, which meant going through all the bureaucracy involved. It was interesting as an education, beginning to deal with people in a professional context, generating the finances and so on. But the basic philosophy was that the context is fifty percent of the work. So that you had to really consider where you were placing the work and how it would do its job there.

AT Context as architectural, social, cultural?

JL There were no parameters set on that, on how you chose to interpret context. In talking about the work it had to be a factor. This freed up the idea of material for me, as it was not about dealing in specific media. It meant that I could choose to work with anything. The emphasis was on the idea rather than on the medium or material, and how that worked conceptually. I could use anything, from a cigarette lighter to a 400-foot piece of plastic. It was entirely up to you. Sculpturally you can really free yourself up if you're not stuck on a specific material.

AT The spaces that you work with, or are interested in creating, are quite psychological. Through the vehicle of music, for example, you seem to be interested in making manifest, concrete, a space that is fairly abstract.

JL I'm always essentially dealing with sculpture. The idea that music can bleed into the work, is nice to me, because I dj and I played in a few bands. But everyone is surrounded with music anyway. It's nice if it bleeds into the work but it's not essential for me – ultimately I am always dealing with sculpture.

I decided to make work with materials that were lying around, that I was interacting with a lot on a day to day basis – cigarettes, sticky tape, really quite basic. I think that's another way that music came in. I have record decks at home so I started using them, also records. They're all just part of the day to day. Whenever I present pieces, I hope that it's something anyone can connect with and recognise – that there's an inroad to the work. Then you can start playing with a psychological and intellectual space after that, but I think it's good if people can immediately connect – it doesn't feel so distant.

AT Thinking about sculpture and the business of making objects, I read something you said in the catalogue for *Tailsliding*: 'There are just too many edges. Rather than create edges, I want to abandon them…Things are not that complicated.'

JL For me with something like *ZOBOP* (pp. 22–25, 122–123), the floor piece, it's creating so many edges that they all dissolve. Is the room expanding or contracting? With the record decks, covering them in glitter pulls all those edges into one idea, it centres them all, and gives them a form of visual escape. Covering an object somehow evaporates the hard edge off the thing, and pulls you towards more of a dreamscape. The hard, day to day, living edge disappears.

AT This dream like quality connects to something else you said: 'I was thinking about spaces between, like the wallpaper, the wall and how you can squeeze yourself into that between space in your head'.

JL Yes, I was thinking about how you read an object when you start thinking about it. How does each person squeeze into that space between an object and your reading of it? With the record decks, you have the objects themselves, then a more abstract, sculptural space below it. For me, that's the psychological space. You're looking at the decks slowly spinning, in a semi hypnotic manner, and then underneath you have that individual space that you enter into. That's where it's happening for me, but the objects underneath... Everyone has their own top layer. I don't mind what you think, as long as you do think...

AT This is clearly reflected in the types of objects that you create. They're visually compelling and have a very specific, almost 'loud' presence, yet they're also fetishised and, in works such as the *psychedelicsoulsticks*, somewhat shamanistic. We're looking at objects that have definite parameters and yet are constantly referring to someplace or something else. It makes them quite transitional.

JL Yes, there's definitely a meditative quality to many of the works, if nothing else through the sheer industry that's involved in making them. All these elements co-exist in any given work, how do we get this release away from this object, while still using the object as a doorway to get away from them, as an escape route. It's your starting point and then you try to get away from the object.

AT Talking about the industry involved in making your pieces, what relationship do you have to the process of making your work?

JL I always make the initial pieces myself. There's no way I know if works are doing that thing for me unless I'm doing them myself. Yet you can't do it all the time and other things come into play. Once I believe that a work is doing what I want it to do, then someone else can, say, put in the floor for example. It just means that they experience that sort of thing. But I'm still setting up that mechanism.

With the floors, I select the colour, the width of the line and outline a basic pattern of alternation. Beyond that, the work makes itself. It's a very simple piece in that respect. You follow the edge of the room, which is basically controlling the piece. You find a rhythm building naturally.

AT In a way, you're the musician but the space is the conductor.

JL Absolutely, the space is totally the conductor. I'd never be able to make the exact same floor twice. It's always interesting to work with the specifics of each space and to follow the suggestions that it offers. Things occur and it's like – wow, I didn't realise that would happen.

AT You mentioned earlier that you work with materials that you interact with on a daily basis. Is there any specific materiality that you seek out when choosing to work with one over another?

JL I wouldn't say that there is anything specific that I'm looking for. More that it's something that I recognise, that I hadn't recognised before, and I see the potential for it. I've had speakers around all my life but didn't know what to do with them until very recently. I knew they were good, but not necessarily what to do with them. It plays on my mind for a while… with the floor, for example, I knew it was a great material but it took me about ten years. I was working as a sign writer and that was the material they used. with *In the Bush* (p. 120), the speaker piece – I'd been thinking about using them for a couple of years, and then just decided quite recently that it would be a good thing to do. It could be anything, maybe one day I'll pick up a cigarette lighter and decide that it would be good to do something with that.

AT In moving from that original idea through to its eventual realisation, do you make any drawings or work with other preparatory elements, or do you go straight to making the work?

JL No. I don't have a studio and tend to work from a sketchbook. But this doesn't involve meticulous drawings, it's more a case of Lambie hyro-glyphics… It's just notes and scrappy drawings, really uninteresting to look at. It's just lines and ideas and notes to myself – remember this etc… It can even be the title of a song. It's all quick notes. Then I decide it's time to make a piece and that means working out how to do it: this invariably involves lots of phoning around, getting hold of people and trying to work out the best way of making it. When I'm preparing for a solo show, I make a lot of the works there, in the gallery. That's an important idea for me, because whether it actually does or doesn't, I believe it brings a particular energy to the works for me. I don't think I've ever made a piece that is sitting ready for six months before a show. I can't work like that. I can sometimes end up not liking stuff that I've had around for a while. It's all very immediate, let's go in and let's do this. I've had these ideas for a while or sometimes even just 10 minutes, and now I really need to go in and do this. Time is collapsed in that respect, in that one push of energy towards the show.

with my recent show at sadie coles, for example, I had no works ready a week before the show opened. Three of the works were actually made in the gallery space – the *psychedelicsoulstick*, *salon unisex* (p. 121) and *Acid perm* (p. 118). The others were constructed over a period of three / four days.

AT The shape of the belts and records in *Acid perm*, as well as the melted shapes on the mirror in *salon unisex*, have a different formal property to works like the more finished speakers.

JL yes, I think that's important to me in a show. I could recognise how formally tight the speakers are and I think it's essential for me that that is offset in a solo show with something that has a different energy, that is more emotional in some way. That's where works like the *psychedelicsoulsticks* or the painted posters come from, really loose and unkempt. I like to think I do that in all my solo shows. It needs that as a balance.

AT your titles are also interesting. some of them are titles of songs for example.

JL some relate directly to the piece itself. For example, *voulez vous* (p. 124) is the title of the record that the wool has been put onto. *Elvis* is just that – a rorschach image of a presley record sleeve. with others, like *weird beard*, it's a name that came up in an internet chat room. It's just things that I pick up when I'm browsing and I make a note of them. These are about bringing something else to the work, creating a texture or ambience about it. They are important for that reason, a title can allow you to enter into another idea. It's good that people then have to juggle that with what they're looking at. It also makes it fun for me.

AT There is a sense of enjoyment, beauty and pleasure in your work, as with all the artists in this exhibition. How important are these notions to you?

JL I enjoy making art.

AT This exhibition posits a loose relationship between sculpture in the 1960s and what's happening today. Do you feel a connection with the work of that period?

JL Of course I look at it, but I look at it all. I'm as interested in that as the next artist. With the speaker pieces, for example, someone mentioned Donald Judd. Maybe somewhere a mile away in the back of my head I can understand that, but I don't start off by thinking I'll make something that relates directly to Judd. I don't make art about art. It's good if someone brings that to the work, that's what I want it to do, I want people to bring their own story, and to take away their own story. But for me it's never a starting point.

AT Looking at what other artist are doing today, and also considering that you've chosen to live in New York, do you feel very strongly connected to a particularly British group of artists, or do you feel affiliations with artists working internationally?

JL Someone asked me this when I moved to New York, whether I considered myself a New York artist. Well, I never considered myself a Glasgow artist. I'm just making work. Again, other people can bring this to it. If critics want to thread something through it all that's great. But for me, it's not a concern. I've never enjoyed shows that lump artists together purely because of geographical location. It's so random, it might as well be 12 artists called David.

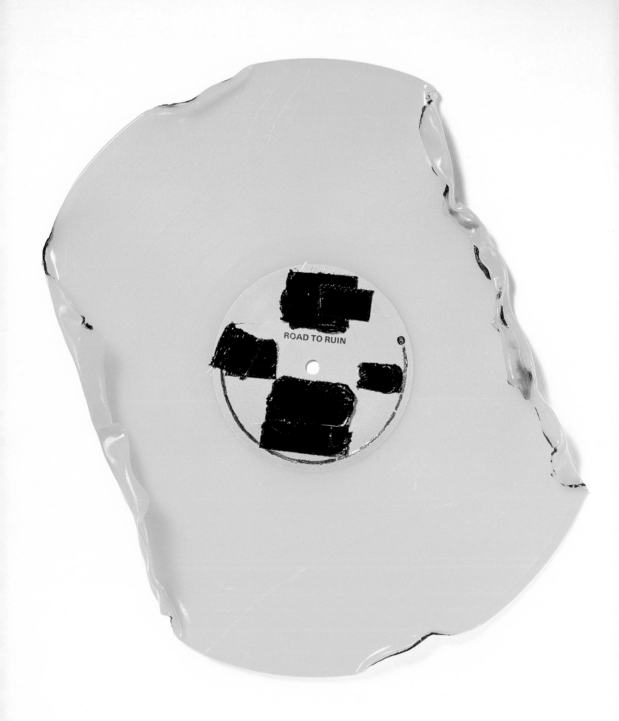

ROAD TO RUIN

Road to Ruin, 2001 opposite
vinyl, record label, gaffer tape
30 x 25 cm
courtesy sadie coles HQ, London and The Modern Institute, Glasgow

groupie, 2001 above
collage on paper
71 x 46 cm
courtesy sadie coles HQ, London and The Modern Institute, Glasgow

Acid Perm, 2002 opposite above
12 and 7 inch records, printed vinyl, belts, tape
210.5 x 275.5 cm
courtesy sadie coles HQ, London and The Modern Institute, Glasgow

weird Glow, 1999 opposite below
Installation view at sadie coles HQ
courtesy sadie coles HQ, London and The Modern Institute, Glasgow

In the bush, 2002   above
speakers, fabric, mirror plexiglas
53.2 x 218.6 x 27.4 cm
courtesy sadie coles HQ, London and The Modern Institute, Glasgow

salon unisex, 2002   opposite
bamboo cane, mirror, glove, bracelets, paint
122 x 81 x 81 cm
courtesy sadie coles HQ, London and The Modern Institute, Glasgow

ZOBOP, 1999 previous pages
Installation view, *voidoid*, Transmission, Glasgow
courtesy sadie coles HQ, London and The Modern Institute, Glasgow

Bed-head, 2002 opposite
Mattress, buttons, thread
50.8 x 190.5 x 94 cm
courtesy sadie coles HQ, London and The Modern Institute, Glasgow

voulez vous, 2001 opposite below
vinyl record, woollen thread
30.5 cm diameter
courtesy sadie coles HQ, London and The Modern Institute, Glasgow

Plaza, 2000 overleaf
Paint, plastic bags
Dimensions variable
courtesy sadie coles HQ, London and The Modern Institute, Glasgow

eva rothschild

Andrea Tarsia Your work moves between two and three dimensions. How do you feel about participating in an exhibition that places an emphasis on sculpture?

Eva Rothschild I never thought of myself as a sculptor, or indeed a painter. If anything I used to think I was a printer, because that's what I spent my degree doing. When I was a student I didn't want to specialise in a specific medium so I went to Belfast, which offered a generic Fine Arts course. It wasn't specialised, your spaces weren't specialised and you found your way into the different areas that you were interested in. I ended up doing a lot of print making, I think because I was interested in the idea of the poster and of fanzines, of putting things out in the public domain. More than anything, I like to think that work shouldn't be limited by any particular discipline. That's something I like about teaching in a sculpture department now. Sculpture has become this wide area, the transsexual of art almost. It can be anything.

AT Your interest in print making can still be felt in your woven posters. Do you make your own images for these or do you use posters that you find?

ER A mixture. Sometimes they're postcards, or photographs, especially of groups of people, groups that are kind of fluid, people on the move. I've also used a lot of op Art patterns, which I draw on computer, and some floral elements. Many of these I collage at first, from magazines and other sources. It's hard to describe what interests me in an individual image. It has to somehow stop me, and make me want to continue that stoppage. They're often images that seem quite banal, but there's something very real in the moment portrayed. I don't feel that they are found images, they're more sought. That's important, the idea that you have to seek and to find, you have to be alert to these things or they pass you by. There are certain images I've used again and again like one of some hunt saboteurs and one of a lotus which was on a plastic bag that I got when I bought a key ring in Australia.

AT The images are rendered in an extraordinary explosion of day-glo. What attracts you to this particular range of colour?

ER I really like day-glo - it's like an extension of black and white, so determined and unlike any other colour. There's also the sense that the colours are relatively new, they have no place in art history. They demand attention, they were made to draw your eye to them first, to almost cancel all other colour. I have tried to make pieces that mix fluorescent with regular colour, and they kill them completely. They are hard to wear – very difficult colours to be human in.

AT They're quite flat, undimensional.

ER Yes, but then occasionally some of them can become quite three-dimensional, which isn't due to the image but about how the colours lie together. It's also very harsh, a short hand for a forcefulness that isn't easy to ignore, while some of the subjects I use are very romantic. I like that mixture. I started using day-glo when I was making the black paint-ings as a contrast. Quiet and loud. They also have similarities with gig posters, the most basic ones with a simple screen print on top of colour. There's definitely a personal enjoyment of them, I'm drawn to them and find them quite compelling.

AT The black of your Perspex structures, on the other hand, acts as a full stop that draws the space around them into them. At the same time they're reflective, which somehow pushes you away. And then they open up through the holes.

ER I want the pieces to be both very present physically and yet difficult to look at as a unified whole, for the viewer to become aware of their own looking in apprehending the work. I am interested in a meditative way of looking where the mind is concentrated on the object but is aiming for something beyond it. This generally occurs in religious settings where the looker has faith and that faith then gives the icon or statue power above and beyond it's materiality. I think it's interesting to relate this older reli-gious way of looking with contemporary western art. I think we furnish our desires with objects and images, it's like we need something tangible to prop up our intangible beliefs.

AT is this what you mean by 'magic minimalism', a phrase I think you coined to describe your work?

ER Yes, although now I've changed it to magic maximalism. I wanted to undo the idea of minimalism as incorruptible, overlapping it with ideas of faith, death, magic, things that are all very messy in a way. I like that idea of corrupting, of scratching the pristine surface. It's like the object tries to be itself but we bring something to it that changes it, a bizarre occultism. Magic and minimalism are opposites in a way; minimalism seemed to be something very definite and clear with real rules, whereas magic, phantasy and mysticism are so grey and so unclear. I really like to try to bring the two together, to undermine and elevate them at the same time.

AT certain objects are more prone to specific readings than others. Do you seek out materials and forms that are very loaded with particular references? I was thinking of works like *Actualisation* (p. 141), made with crystal balls, or the triangular, pyramid-like shape of works like *Black Ruin* or *Bad Hat* (p. 138).

ER *Actualisation* came out of a previous work, *Visualisation*, which is made up of different images. The title refers to the belief that visualising what you want to happen will make it happen. I had all these New Age posters which I had begun to photograph in black and white. I was a little embarrassed by them and couldn't really figure out how to show them without them appearing simply novel or corny, yet I wanted them to be seen as I felt that they had some significance. They were all different yet all the same, in that they were of a genre with a clear and known iconography. I matched the posters with drawings, which isolated elements from the printed images, then added some non-fantasy images that seemed to show the same thing. I felt that together all of the images were about visualising and really trying to bring into existence a world that isn't there.

Those two terms, visualisation and actualisation, are at the core of the things we do as artists. You think, visualise something, and then you actualise it. you want to see it and you have to make it, you want it to exist. I made *Actualisation* to go with *visualisation* and I felt that one was just another manifestation of the other. I think that's actually the case with quite a lot of art work, you're doing the same thing over and over and then you realise they're all variations on the same theme. It's not about versions, it's more that you want to see how something can exist in different states, like a ghost taking on different forms.

AT on a very practical level, talking about actualisation, what's the process that leads from an idea to making it happen?

ER I make quite a few drawings, on the computer and by hand. with works like the woven pieces there is a certain format, so once I get into it the process kind of makes the work. They inform the other works, in that making them is quite methodical, trance-like. of course there are decisions that you need to make, but these are basic and quite limited: either over or under. It's very binary at that point, almost a case of right or wrong. which I like, because the results aren't like that.

I tend to go backwards and forwards in making a work. I draw, I read a lot, often the same things again and again, and then sometimes I make some small paintings, then I ignore them for a while. I weave in and out of each work. I make things which are like physical sketches in some way, that need to be around on the edge of my consciousness for a while and then I sort of swoop in and pull them into existing in a more definite way. The head pieces are interesting to me because they stay in an incomplete state, they're almost existing, and there could always be more work done on them. They're very reticent.

The perspex sculptures need a lot of planning and have to be a certain size, partly because for me it's to do with a tension between a sculpture and a knick-knack - I made a piece once called *knick-knack*. we have all these objects that don't really do anything, crystals, lava lamps even flowers, they don't function in any clear way. They are things that we separate out from the world and assign a specificity to. The same is true of posters. This action of looking and choosing and separating is important.

It's about realising that an object or image, despite having no defined function, does interact with us in some way, does allow us an experience that we don't get anywhere else. This is as true of a 'knick-knack' as it is of a Picasso.

AT Some of your works are hand crafted while others are made from mass produced elements. This runs parallel to a formal contrast between, for example, the looseness of fringes and the rigidity of Perspex.

ER I like there to be differences in the materials and methods I use, for the works to be created in different ways. It's like they can fill different criteria, they allow each other to be different parts of the same thing. I like using craft methods for some of the works because it aligns them so closely with me as the maker. Craft is something that has been sanitised by mass production, the hand-crafted object has become a symbol of quality and luxury whereas craft techniques actually sprung from real necessity. I want to try to bring some of that toughness back to the crafted object, to make something both homespun and hardcore. The Perspex is reflective and perforated; this means that although the pieces have a strong physical presence, there is a sense in which their material-ity is untrustworthy. The edges are so shiny that it is hard to tell where one plane ends and another begins. This uncertainty about edges is even more explicit in the woven pieces, where there are two or more images within the same work. They're both equal in the piece, one isn't the back-ground to the other because they have to overlap and co-exist. I've used fringes a lot with the hangings and the leather pieces, because they con-tinue the confusion over where the piece actually ends and begins physically.

AT You've mentioned elements of New Age and Romanticism in your work. These often come together in some of your titles, as well as in images that possess the quality of 1960s and 70s psychedelia. What's your interest in these areas?

ER I think there's a general belief that the current interest in what's called New Age originated in the '60s. While that was definitely a moment when it reached a critical mass, spirituality and searching have always been part of Romanticism. Think of Byron, coleridge, Blake, Yeats....The 60s were important because this was when large numbers of kids who were expected to form the backbone of American society decided to really experiment with alternative ways of living. Mass availability of psychedelic drugs also led to a period of simultaneous, instantaneous 'self-awareness' and 'spiritual awakening'. It's easy to write off that period, it's naivety and excess, but politically it has had a hugely positive impact on society. It is incredible to think that at that time young people really felt that they could change the world. unfortunately I think that the emphasis placed on being free to do your own thing within the 'movement' imploded on itself. The elevation of individual desire over the communal is something that has become an absolute cornerstone of advanced capitalism, in a way that true hippies would be horrified by. The thing that really saddens me about the 60s is that young people are practically beaten round the head with both it's failures and successes as a way of disparaging contemporary youth culture and their desire for a different world.

The idea of an individual path is central to New Age practice and is probably one of the reasons for its popularity today. unlike traditional religions, with their rules, dogma and emphasis on consequences for actions taken, New Age offers a spirituality without censure. It concentrates on the needs of the individual and their fulfilment and it doesn't cast the practitioner as the subject of a demanding god in the way most religions do. I am not an expert in this area and I don't want to disparage other people's beliefs. But I am interested in the desire for faith and in how we dabble in the alternative spiritualities that New Age has thrown up. New Age has cornered it's market so successfully, there are shops on every suburban corner groaning under the weight of crystals and dream catchers and power-bracelets and other quasi-spiritual knick-knacks. what are they? what do we want from them? Do we believe they will help us?

AT so you're particularly interested in the desire for that belief. And desire today is no longer turned inwards – it's out there and played out to the extreme. It seems to be geared towards achieving a state of hyperconsciousness, or extra-consciousness.

ER yes, I guess it's quite a romantic idea, but I think that aesthetically I want to have a tough take on what seems a soft subject. For me there is an idealism in this desire that rather than being wistful and dreamy can be forceful and demanding. It's more about wanting a different world and being willing to pursue that through protest and transformation than through aromatherapy and horoscopes.

In some ways it's about trying not to fill a gap, but to show that the gap is there in contemporary culture where everything is available and catered for. It's like trying to supply something else that doesn't fulfil a specific need, but that might just lead to the next question. I'm not really interested in the answers. I'm more interested in the continuation and expansion of the search.

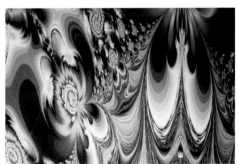

source material courtesy the artist p.128 and above

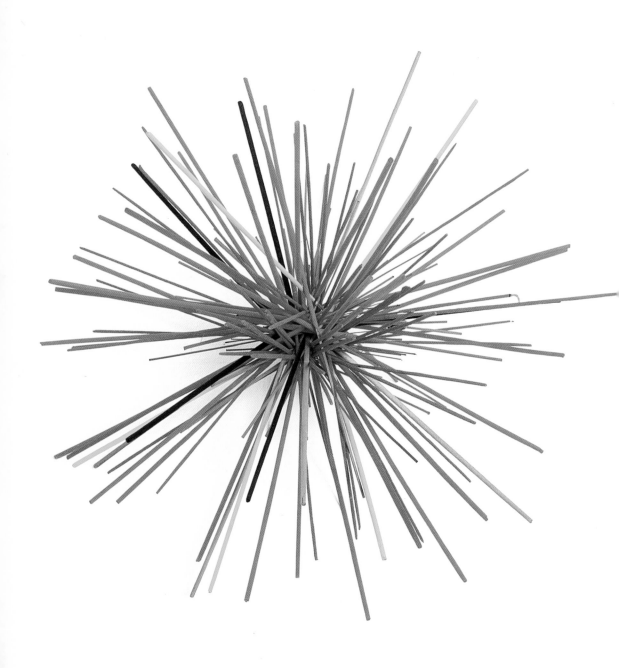

N.G.O., 2002 previous page left
Leather strips
Dimensions variable
courtesy Modern Art, London and The Modern Institute, Glasgow

Bad Hat, 2002 previous page right
Perspex
Dimensions variable
courtesy Modern Art, London and The Modern Institute, Glasgow

Disappearer, 2001 opposite
Incense sticks
Dimensions variable
courtesy Modern Art, London and The Modern Institute, Glasgow

Actualisation, 1998 above
crystal balls and stands
Dimensions variable
courtesy Modern Art, London and The Modern Institute, Glasgow

Free Jazz (1), 2002 previous page left
woven poster and vinyl
190 x 83 cm
courtesy Modern Art, London and The Modern Institute, Glasgow

Rhythm and knowledge, 2001 previous page right
woven poster
230 x 230 cm
commissioned by The showroom, London
courtesy Modern Art, London and The Modern Institute, Glasgow
Photo: Daniel Brooke

I and I, 2000 opposite
woven poster
119 x 84 cm
courtesy Modern Art, London and The Modern Institute, Glasgow

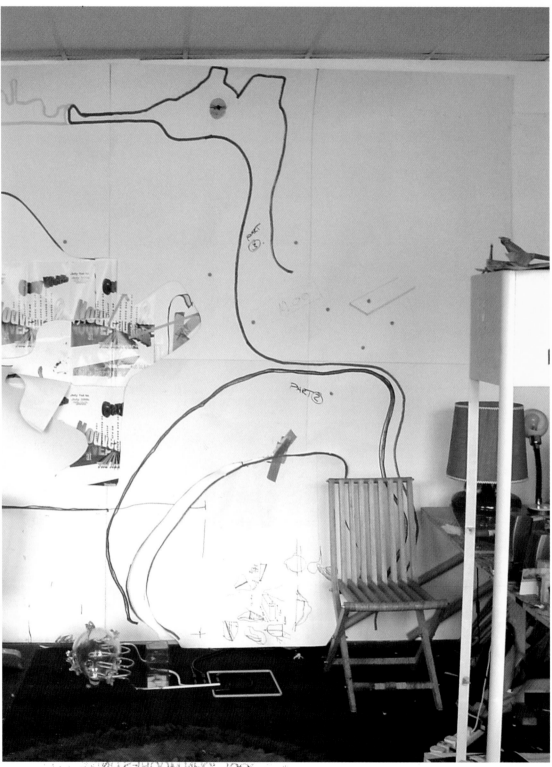

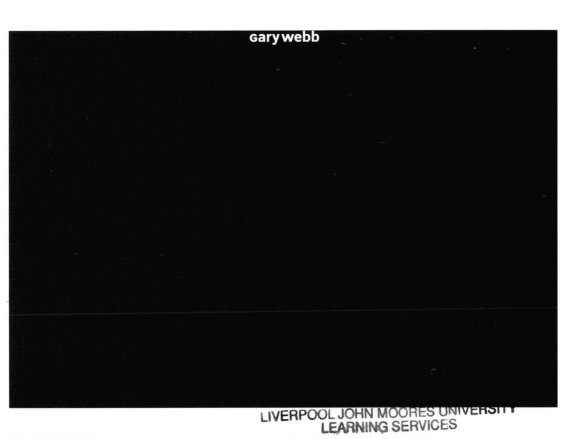

gary webb

iwona blazwick does the definition of sculpture have a meaning for you – is it still relevant?

gary webb no not really – if you were a sculptor you'd be using one material in a way which is maybe more the essence, or idea of making sculpture... i'm kind of in the middle between sculpture and painting.

IB over the last 10 years artists have been creating installations or tableaux which propose that you are entering some kind of parallel world. there has also been an engagement with site, work generated by its context. in contrast your practice seems to have an abstract, hermetic, almost centrifugal force about it, its components relate to eachother not to an external context.

GW A lot of the work goes back in on itself. it seems to have a personal relationship with me...

IB you combine found objects with materials that you have either made yourself or commissioned; sound can also be a component. why do you combine these elements?

GW The objects i've brought in seem to be more symbolic than the objects i make or get specifically shaped or chromed... otherwise the work would just go off and become so abstract, it needs some kind of reality, these things that you really do see every day and deal with and that you know very well. it seems silly to ignore them, i enjoy them both having a part.

IB do you see their associations lying in every day experience or are they about triggering unconscious, intuitive connections?

GW A lot of the drawings are very much hand to paper, no connections, no relationships. some are based on very vivid moments of waking up in the middle of the night with the image of exactly what you are making, like some odd religious experience. This image flashes in front of you, you get the colours and everything all at the same time and if you are quick enough you can remember it and then draw it and make it.

IB when you go out and get things do you have something in mind, or do you let yourself find things by accident?

GW I'll walk around doing some shopping or something, and there'll be a small part in a shop. I'll take it home and it'll go on the side and hang around for a bit. Then something else will go on and I'll see it on the other side of the room and put it together; it will have a history and relationships, a story to tell for itself. You put them together and the stories get more and more mangled and something starts happening. Maybe it becomes so much emptiness...

IB There are lots of formal plays of transparency and reflection and very vivid juxtapositions of colour. How do you make those decisions?

GW Probably autistically! It takes me eight months to think about it and a week to get it firm in my mind what it's going to be... The shaping of everything is very difficult but the choice of colours – there's not enough in the world in some ways for you to choose.

IB Does a work grow organically, or do you have a complete image in your mind that you set out to build?

GW *Paranoidmountain* (p. 168–169) started with a drawing... but when the drawing was first made it was nothing like the end result... certain shapes need a certain structure... some works will get made like the drawings, then they'll sit and I'll look at them and know they need a bit of gold chain or a bit of blue paint on the floor or something. It just seems to unbalance it again.

IB A piece called *Heart and soul* (p. 9, 160–161) uses neon; because it's a medium for signage your eye is immediately attracted to 'reading' it for information or a name; but it's completely abstract. This sense of teasing and frustrating comprehension runs through all the work...

GW I like that. I find that quite an intense place to be involved in – when you're trying to avoid the situation where you can say – it looks like this. I love avoiding being caught for any reasons of language.

IB what part does the sound play?

GW sometimes I get a bit angry with the works in that you go off and make them and you're left with this material. It's not personal enough. You don't want sound in every one and have some sort of system – but some of them need it just to up the personal level – where the materials are just not doing enough. There's nice colours and there's great glass and there's wood and stuff, but the materials can't talk to you – you need the sound to just talk to you a bit.

IB The titles add yet another component to the work.

GW I don't like to have anything untitled – there's so much stuff that's gone into them – *Been there seen it and done it* was just an old slang saying of my dad's. *white city* was amazing, making this condensed pink world and then suddenly finding out that the BBC came from white city. I also love black music. They're all very personal things. I had a landlord called Rob Little and he was quite a small guy so I made this thing called *Mr Little Tree* (p. 167).

IB Is there a Bucks Fizz song title in there somewhere?

GW In all of them!

IB where did you study?

GW I went to Bournemouth and Pool college and ended up doing drama, a bit of fashion design and graphics. Then I went off and did three years of foundation courses – I did furniture for 3 weeks and hated the whole thing. Then someone said – do you know of Fine Art and I went, no what's that? I said you have to be dead don't you to do it? And it was just amazing, that was it for me – just to be able to go and do some drawing or bend some metal or do some screen printing… that was a very important thing - to do everything. I tried more specific things before like graphics – it's a type of being that I knew I couldn't be. I think that you find this art thing – you realise in some strange way that you're able to do everything else. I wanted to do this thing that I really didn't understand.

IB some of the artists in our show went to Glasgow school of Art; they've talked about how influential the Environmental Department was because it questioned what sculpture, environment or installation actually were. what department were you studying in?

GW I was in the visual Art department at Goldsmiths where you go and sit in the space and that's it, you are left to do what you want. To me that was absolutely perfect. on the other side, there was this incredibly dense theoretical stuff, like Deleuze and Lacan, that I'd never heard before, it was a whole new breed of language. I'd never read, but just to sit and listen was so fulfilling for me. It was easy for me to go off and make work because I didn't read or write anything anyway. so I listened and spent my time making the work. But I never got crushed by any kind of relationship with language.

IB A lot of what you do seems to me to have echoes in modernist strategies.

GW I don't really know enough about the history of art but I think there are relationships with previous things. when I was looking at the 1960s sculpture at Tate Britain I really found a different presence - the work is made with one colour, it feels very impersonal, to have a relationship with the outside world. I've definitely grown up with a relationship with huge indoor shopping malls, indoor drive-in areas, indoor everything.

IB I suppose a revolutionary aspect of that work is the way it brought pure colour and abstract form into sculpture. In the same way I feel that you use colour as a sculptural medium - it's 3 dimensional, tangible. It also reminds me of Donald Judd in the way he uses Perspex where colour is not applied, but is intrinsic to the material. He also subcontracted the manufacture of his work – how do you commission the components of your works?

GW It's simple because there are individual people that do individual things. I get this piece of rock and there's this eyehole thing that has to go on the end and that will be done by the welding guy and that's all he does; it will then be taken to the dip moulding guy and so on - that's what they're set up to do all day long. When you head towards the crafts area that becomes tricky; they tend to think, I'm not going to make something for another artist, I am an artist. I like pushing that area, it's an argumentative one, even in the process of manufacturing.

IB So you work out the specification in advance, as a drawing?

GW For example the glass thing in *paranoidmountain* – I'll say, just blob this to upturn over there and he'll have sculpted this block. I love when they do their own thing, the chance element in it – they've bent it to an angle other than in the drawing. In some pieces the people who have made a part have signed it, I really like that, it opens things up - in the end the trace of the artist is in some ways lost.

IB You can't see these works in one position; they're very imagistic but you have to keep walking around them because things are seen through or reflected in other things revealing completely different perspectives and sculptural relationships. Do you know that in advance?

GW Yes, there's definitely a use of certain materials to give that freedom of viewing. It doesn't make it so 'this is what it is'. I find it kind of sexy to walk behind something and not be seen for a little bit – it's a bit romantic behind the back of something. Then you can come around to the front and see everything.

IB For your installation at the Whitechapel Gallery, you're creating transparent soft plastic islands for the works to sit on.

GW It's to remove it from the idea of being just sculpture – to place things onto another floor of your own. similar colour and material seems to be enough just to set itself back a bit.

IB The works are separated off so they become autonomous; but they're united by these 'modular' islands made of triangular cells, that connect together. They remind me of Buckminster Fuller's geodesic domes, these kinds of '60s systems – both architectural and molecular. Your work does seem to hover between pop cultural forms and organic shapes – for example in *paranoidmountain* the seahorse combines the natural world with 1950s ornamentation....

GW I want to go towards the feeling of a Philip Guston painting, and the weird world of the 20th century and the colours, symbols and shapes of 2002.

IB The works are also very shiny, perfect and quite synthetic.

GW When you get up close to them they're not as well made as they seem, they have an air of having been made 20 years ago, like the way the joins don't really work; I would like to introduce more of that crappiness. In some ways there's not a full quality charge like the Bloomberg building or something.

IB You mentioned being exposed to the ideas that were coming out of theory in the 1990s which may have touched on things like psychoanalysis, cultural or social theory. Are you interested in exploring theoretical or political issues in the work?

GW I think there are political levels to the work but they're not issues that jump out at you. There is definitely frustration in there about capital and environmental problems, like pollution. These materials all come out of mass-production – where does it all go, where does it all end up, all the chemicals and oils that are used to produce this stuff?

cock and bull, 2001 opposite
plastic, assorted metals, wood, perspex, china bowls
184 x 135 x 46 cm
courtesy The British Council, London

Heart and soul, 2000 overleaf
Glass and neon
100 x 31 cm
courtesy Anita and Poju zabludowicz, London

screws can be bullets, 2001-2002 opposite
perspex, various materials, wood, paint, mini-disk, card, clay, plastic
84 x 147.5 x 69 cm
courtesy The Approach, London

coming home, 2002 overleaf
plastic-coated metal, resin, perspex, sand, paint, herbs
190 x 201 x 201 cm
courtesy The Approach, London

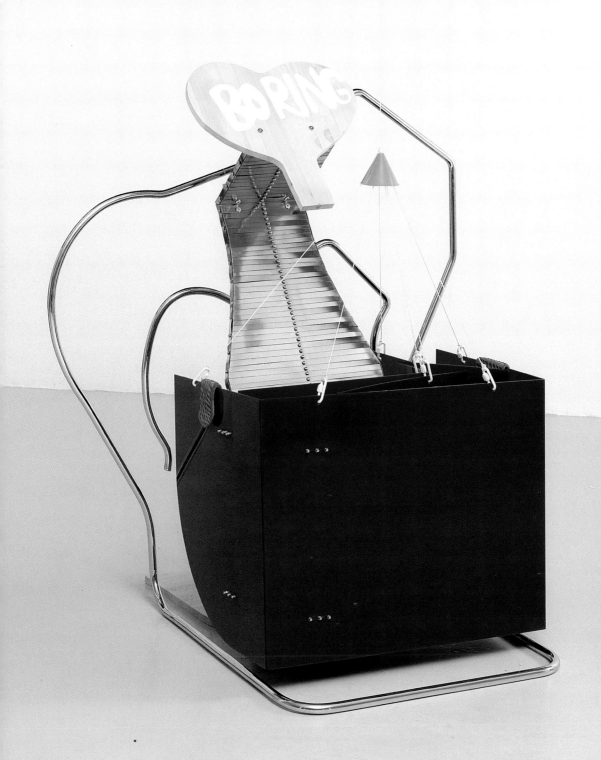

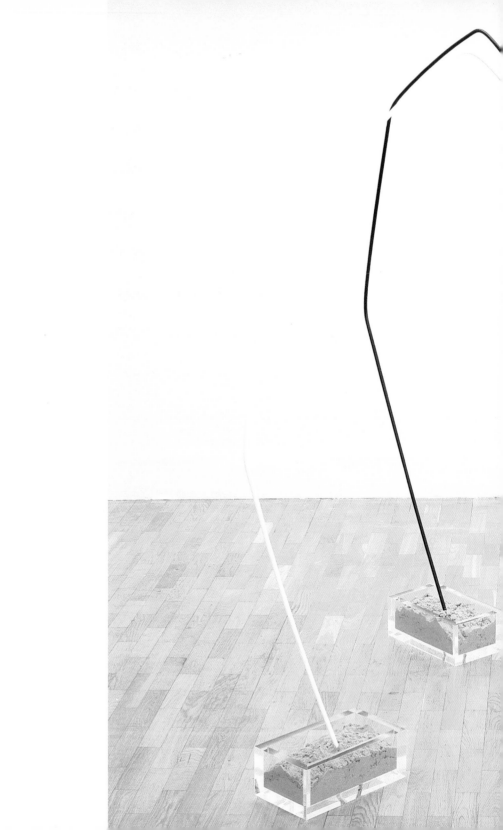

Mumdadland, 1997 opposite
Q-cell, plywood, aluminium, spray paint, plastic, paper
108 x 193 x 109 cm
courtesy The Approach, London

Mr Little Tree, 1997 above
Mixed media, walkman and cassette
137 x 120 x 84 cm
courtesy The Approach, London

Paranoidmountain, 2001 overleaf
steel, Perspex, glass, sprayed Q-cell, wood, mini-disc and speaker
215 x 121 x 204 cm
private collection
courtesy The Approach, London

shahin afrassiabi

born 1969, lives and works in London
education 1995–1997 MA visual arts,
goldsmiths college, London

solo exhibitions

2002 vilma gold, London
2000 *you're a heavenly thing*, vilma gold,
London

group exhibitions

2002 *early one morning*, whitechapel art
gallery, London
early one morning display in conjunction with
tra-La-La: british sculpture in the sixties,
tate britain, London
2001 *beck's Futures*, institute of contemporary
arts, London; sotheby's, new york (cat)
just history, tal esther gallery, tel aviv
cover versions, the trade apartment, London
2000 *eventa 5*, uppsala, sweden
the songs I like, michael janssen gallery,
cologne
wreck of Hope, the nunnery, London
wooden heart, avco, London
these epic islands, vilma gold, London
1999 *hundreds of thousands*, the trade
apartment, London
cluster bomb, morrison judd, London
1998 *surfacing*, institute of contemporary arts,
London
printemps, deutsch britische freundschaft,
London
the powder room, factorij 63, rotterdam
1997 *Humdrum (red)*, the trade apartment,
London
1995 group exhibition, 20 dean street, London

awards

2000 individual artist grant, London arts board

claire barclay

born 1968, lives and works in glasgow
education 1991–1993 MA glasgow school of art

solo exhibitions

2002 *some reddish work done at night*,
doggerfisher, edinburgh
2001 *welcome for sea and game*, bulkhead,
glasgow
2000 *Homemaking*, moderna museet projekt,
stockholm (cat)
take to the ground, the showroom, London
1998 *dream catcher*, 200 gertrude street,
melbourne, australia
1997 *out of the woods*, centre for contemporary
art, glasgow
1996 *museum intervention*, tasmanian museum
and art gallery
claire barclay, new works, plimsoll gallery,
centre for the arts, Hobart, tasmania
1994 *claire barclay, new works*, transmission,
glasgow

group exhibitions

2002 *early one morning*, whitechapel art
gallery, London
early one morning display in conjunction with
tra-La-La: british sculpture in the sixties,
tate britain, London
any where, centre for curatorial studies,
bard college, new york
2001 *Here and now*, dundee contemporary arts
(cat)
G3 NY, casey kaplan gallery, new york
circles, zentrum für kunst und
medientechnologie, karlsruhe
2000 *If I ruled the world: part 2*, centre for
contemporary arts, glasgow
bush mechanics, collaboration with ann ooms,
catalyst arts, belfast
1999 *If I ruled the world*, Living art museum,
reykjavik

A still volcano life, exhibition with cathy wilkes, south gallery, sydney

1998-99 *Glasgow 99*, Govanhill millenium park project

1998 *seeing Hozomeen*, collective gallery, edinburgh

Nettverk Glasgow, museet for samtidkunst, oslo

1997 *Hong Kong Island*, transmission, Glasgow

1995 *Exchange Resources*, catalyst arts, belfast

Taking Form, fruitmarket gallery, edinburgh

1994 *The Institute of cultural Anxiety*, Institute for contemporary arts, london (cat)

Art unlimited: multiples of the 60s and 90s, centre for contemporary arts, Glasgow; The south Bank centre, london (cat)

1992 *Invisible cities*, fruitmarket gallery, edinburgh

Jim Lambie

Born 1964, lives and works in New York and Glasgow

Education 1990-1994 Glasgow school of art

solo exhibitions

2003 MOMA, oxford

2002 Inverleith House, edinburgh

salon unisex, sadie coles HQ, london

Gale Gates et al, brooklyn museum of art, New York

2001 *Jim Lambie*, Jack Hanley, san francisco

Jim Lambie, The Modern Institute, Glasgow

2000 Triangle, paris

solo project, konrad fischer, dusseldorf

1999 *weird Glow*, sadie coles HQ, london

voidoid, transmission, Glasgow

ZOBOP, The showroom, london

Group exhibitions

2002 *Early one Morning*, whitechapel art Gallery, london

Early one Morning display in conjunction with *Tra-la-la: British sculpture in the sixties*, Tate Britain, london

Electric Dreams, barbican, london

My Head is on Fire but my Heart is Full of Love, charlottenberg museum, copenhagen (cat)

2001 *Painting at the Edge of the world*, walker art center, minneapolis (cat)

Here and Now, Dundee contemporary arts (cat)

Tailsliding, British council touring show (cat)

2000 *off the Record*, bucknell art Gallery of pennsylvania

Body-space net and other creations, kunsthalle Basel

Dream Machines, Dundee contemporary arts; mappin art Gallery; camden arts centre, london (cat)

sadie coles, Hoxton HQ, london

what If, moderna museet, stockholm

THE BRITISH ART SHOW 5, EDINBURGH, CARDIFF,
BIRMINGHAM, SOUTHAMPTON (CAT)
BLACK GLOSS, ANTON KERN, NEW YORK
1999 GROUP SHOW, GALERIE KRINZINGER, VIENNA
PAPERMAKE, MODERN ART INC., LONDON
CREEPING REVOLUTION, FOKSAL GALLERY, WARSAW
HEART AND SOUL, 60 LONG LANE, LONDON
THE QUEEN IS DEAD, STILLS GALLERY,
EDINBURGH (CAT)
1998 *LOVECRAFT*, SPACEX GALLERY, EXETER
THE MODERN INSTITUTE @ SADIE COLES, SADIE COLES
HQ, LONDON
HOST, TRAMWAY, GLASGOW
1997 *EUROPEAN COUPLES AND OTHERS*,
TRANSMISSION, GLASGOW
1996 *GIRLS HIGH*, FRUITMARKET GALLERY, EDINBURGH
INSANESTUPIDPHATFUCTPERVERT, CUBITT STREET,
LONDON; CONCRETE SKATES, GLASGOW
ART FOR PEOPLE, TRANSMISSION, GLASGOW
1995 *IN STEREO*, TRANSMISSION, GLASGOW

COMMISSIONS AND AWARDS

2000 PAUL HAMLYN FOUNDATION AWARD FOR ARTISTS,
LONDON
1998 BRITISH COUNCIL AWARD TOWARDS RESIDENCY AT
TRIANGLE, MARSEILLE
THE MODERN INSTITUTE 'ULTRALOW' COMMISSION

EVA ROTHSCHILD

BORN 1971, LIVES AND WORKS IN LONDON
EDUCATION 1997–1999 MA GOLDSMITH'S COLLEGE,
LONDON
1990–1993 BA, UNIVERSITY OF ULSTER, BELFAST

SOLO EXHIBITIONS

2002 *EVA ROTHSCHILD*, PROJECT ART GALLERY, DUBLIN
EVA ROTHSCHILD, MODERN ART, LONDON
2001 *PEACEGARDEN*, THE SHOWROOM, LONDON;
CORNERHOUSE, MANCHESTER (CAT)
EVA ROTHSCHILD, FRANCESCA KAUFFMAN GALLERY,
MILAN
1999 *EVA ROTHSCHILD*, THE MODERN INSTITUTE,
GLASGOW
1997 *GREAT WALL/BLACK HOLE*, IAIN IRVING PROJECTS,
ABERDEENSHIRE
1996 *EVA ROTHSCHILD*, CENTRE FOR CONTEMPORARY
ART, GLASGOW
1995 *EVA ROTHSCHILD*, BERCSENYI GALLERIA,
BUDAPEST, HUNGARY

GROUP EXHIBITIONS

2002 *EARLY ONE MORNING*, WHITECHAPEL ART
GALLERY, LONDON
EARLY ONE MORNING DISPLAY IN CONJUNCTION WITH
TRA-LA-LA: BRITISH SCULPTURE IN THE SIXTIES,
TATE BRITAIN, LONDON
ELECTRIC DREAMS, BARBICAN, LONDON
MY HEAD IS ON FIRE BUT MY HEART IS FULL OF LOVE,
CHARLOTTENBERG MUSEUM, COPENHAGEN (CAT)
2001 *SILHOUETTES AND CUT-OUTS*, LENBACHAUS,
MUNICH
TATTOO SHOW, MODERN ART, LONDON
BROWN, THE APPROACH, LONDON
TAILSLIDING, BRITISH COUNCIL TOURING SHOW (CAT)
PRODIGAL PRODIGY, WHITE BOX, NEW YORK (CAT)
2000 *PERFIDY*, KETTLES YARD, CAMBRIDGE; CONVENT
OF LA TOURETTE, EVEUX
TONIGHT, THE MODERN INSTITUTE, GLASGOW
COMES THE SPIRIT…, JERWOOD SPACE, LONDON
PROPER, CENTRE FOR CONTEMPORARY ART, VILNIUS,
LITHUANIA

dream machines, dundee contemporary arts;
mappin art gallery; camden arts centre,
london (cat)
1999 *utopias*, douglas hyde gallery, dublin
high red centre, centre for contemporary art,
glasgow
1998 *seeing hozomeen*, collective gallery,
edinburgh
crystal state, 3 month gallery, liverpool
1997 *dialogue*, w139, amsterdam
european couples, transmission, glasgow
1996 *art for people*, transmission, glasgow
into the void, ikon gallery, birmingham

commissions and awards
2000 delfina trust studio residency
2000–2002–06
camden arts centre, london, artist in residence
1997 PADT/BAA heathrow arts programme,
belfast lounge commission

gary webb
born 1973, lives and works in london
education 1994–1997 BA goldsmiths college,
london

solo exhibitions
2000 *nouveau riche*, with keith farquhar, the
approach, london
1998 *gary webb plays gary webb*, the approach,
london

group exhibitions
2002 *early one morning*, whitechapel art
gallery, london
early one morning display in conjunction with
tra-la-la: british sculpture in the sixties,
tate britain, london
the young and the hung, galerie thaddaeus
ropac, salzburg
2001 *tailsliding*, british council touring
exhibition (cat)
casino 2001, SMAK, ghent (cat)
dedalic convention: du und ich, with liam
gillick, kunstverein, salzburg
brown, the approach, london
haemorrhaging of states, TENT, rotterdam
2000 *heart and soul*, sandroni rey gallery, los
angeles
insanity benefit, vilma gold, london
abstract art, delfina, london
1999 *heart and soul*, 60 long lane, london
newbuild, platform, london
oldnewtown, casey kaplan gallery, new york
1998 *die young stay pretty*, institute of
contemporary arts, london (cat)

awards
2000 delfina trust, studio residency,
2000–2002

early one morning

Lower Gallery
Gary Webb
cock and Bull, 2001
plastic, assorted metals, wood, perspex,
china bowls
184 x 135 x 46 cm
The British council

Gary Webb
Heart and soul, 2000
glass and neon
100 x 31.5 cm
Anita and Poju Zabludowicz

Gary Webb
Paranoidmountain, 2001
steel, perspex, glass, sprayed Q-cell,
wood, speakers
350 x 250 x 300 cm
Private collection, London

Gary Webb
coming Home, 2002
plastic coated metal, resin, perspex, sand,
paint, herbs
190 x 201 x 201 cm
courtesy The Approach, London

Gary Webb
Mirage of Loose change, 2001
chrome, steel, plastic, granite, wood, neon
108 x 132 x 47 cm
Arts council collection, Hayward gallery,
London

Gary Webb
sound of the Blue Light, 2002
Marble, copper, wood, paper, graphite,
perspex, speaker, CD player
184 x 356 x 257 cm
courtesy The Approach, London

Gary Webb
Matte Module, 2002
series of rubber mats
70 x 70 x 70 cm
courtesy The Approach, London

claire Barclay
collars for woodseers, 2002
Mixed media
Dimensions variable
courtesy the artist and Doggerfisher, Edinburgh

New Gallery
shahin Afrassiabi
Floor, 2002
Mixed media
Dimensions variable
courtesy the artist and Vilma Gold, London

shahin Afrassiabi
Display with Table, 2002
Mixed media
Dimensions variable
courtesy the artist and Vilma Gold, London

Upper Gallery
shahin Afrassiabi
Display with Linoleum Tiles, 2002
Mixed media
Dimensions variable
courtesy the artist and Vilma Gold, London

shahin Afrassiabi
shelf Display with clock Radio, 2002
Mixed media
Dimensions variable
courtesy the artist and Vilma Gold, London

shahin Afrassiabi
Amp, 2002
chromograph
56.3 x 74.5 x 3.2 cm
courtesy the artist and Vilma Gold, London

List of works

Eva Rothschild
Nun, 2002
Acrylic on Perspex
38 x 20.5 x 1.5 cm
Courtesy The Modern Institute, Glasgow

Eva Rothschild
Hothouse, 2002
Leather and mixed media
Dimensions variable
Courtesy Modern Art, London

Eva Rothschild
Midnight, 2002
Wood, leather
Each 190 x 60 cm
Courtesy The Modern Institute, Glasgow

Eva Rothschild
2 x *Guides*, 2002
Woven paper
Each 44 x 54 cm
Private collection

Eva Rothschild
Early Learning, 2002
Rosewood, crystal, leather
Dimensions variable
Courtesy The Modern Institute, Glasgow

Eva Rothschild
Disappearer, 1998 – 2002
Incense sticks
Dimensions variable
Courtesy The Modern Institute, Glasgow

Eva Rothschild
within you, without you II, 2002
Perspex
300 x 147 x 118 cm
Courtesy The Modern Institute, Glasgow

Eva Rothschild
Equal and Equal, 2002
Woven paper
250 x 200 cm
Courtesy Modern Art, London

Jim Lambie
ZOBOP, 2002
Gold, silver, black and white vinyl tape
Dimensions variable
Private collection

Jim Lambie
Tandoori Nights, 2002
Alice bands and gaffer tape
109 x 76 x 50 cm
Courtesy Sadie Coles HQ, London and The
Modern Institute, Glasgow

Jim Lambie
venom wild pitch, 2002
Belt
54 x 104 x 4 cm
Courtesy Sadie Coles HQ, London and The
Modern Institute, Glasgow

Jim Lambie
shampoo and Rinse, 2002
Mirrors, paint
60 x 78 x 3 cm
Courtesy Sadie Coles HQ, London and The
Modern Institute, Glasgow

Jim Lambie
Erotic Discount, 2002
Bamboo cane, glove, paint and buttons
119.5 x 77 cm
Private collection

Jim Lambie
warm sand, 2002
Paper
9.5 x 46 x 3 cm
Courtesy Sadie Coles HQ, London and The
Modern Institute, Glasgow

Lenders

The artists, Arts council collection, The British council, Sadie coles HQ, London, Doggerfisher, Edinburgh, Modern Art, London, The Approach, London, The Modern Institute, Glasgow, Vilma Gold, London, Anita and Poju Zabludowicz And those who wish to remain anonymous

with special thanks to the following for their invaluable support of this exhibition
**Henry Moore
Foundation**
Whitechapel circle of Friends, Shane Akeroyd

chairman of the Trustees
Keir McGuinness

Whitechapel Trustees
**Duncan Ackery, Jan Debbaut, Lex Fenwick, Michael Keith, John Newbigin
Dominic Palfreyman, Niru Ratnam, Alice Rawsthorn, Andrea Rose**

Whitechapel Director
Iwona Blazwick

Whitechapel staff
John Baker, Beth Chaplin, Kate Crane, Alison Digance, David Gleeson, Katie Harding, Janeen Haythornthwaite, Dorothea Jaffé, Annabel Johnson, Victoria Jones, Helen Lloyd, Thomas Malcherczyk, Rachel Mapplebeck, Alicia Miller, Warren Morley, Rebecca Morrill, Raksha Patel, Jill Porter, Demitra Procopiou, Christy Robson, Emma Speight, Anthony Spira, Candy Stobbs, Andrea Tarsia, Simon Wigginton, Nayia Yiakoumaki

Published by Whitechapel Art Gallery
Distributed by
Cornerhouse Publications
70 Oxford Street
Manchester M1 5NH
Tel: +44 (0)161 200 1503
Fax: +44 (0)161 200 1504

Front cover
Heather McDonough